Prison Walls to Waterfalls

Foreword.

I'd like to Dedicate this book to my late father who was a massive influence in my life and is sorely missed.

Les Duncan 1947-2022.

Always my Hero.

Rest in peace Dad, Stand Easy.

Also to the many colleagues I served with who have since passed over.

To the ones still slogging away in Jails and former colleagues who have left the service

Please stay safe and well.

I'd like to thank James McDonald for his help and advice in writing this book.

Also my partner Sarah for enduring my endless typing.

The book describes accounts and memories of incidents that happened during my career with HMPS.

Tony Duncan . 2022

Some Abbreviations used.

Cat A- Category A Prisoner or Prison.

SSU- Special Secure Unit.
A unit housing Exceptional Risk Category A Prisoners.

Seg- Segregation Unit.

The Block-Also the Segregation Unit.
Also known as " The Chokey"

Bang Up- Locking up.

Shipped out- Transferred.

Ghosted- Moved to another Prison.

DST- Dedicated Search Team.

MUFTI- Minimum Use of Force and Tactical unit.

SO- Senior Officer.

PO- Principal Officer.

OSG- Operational Support Grade.

C and R- Control and Restraint.

Res- Residential Unit.

Hooch- Prisoners home brew.

Dirty Protest- Prisoner covers themselves and or their Cell in faeces.

Nicking- Placing a Prisoner on Governors report under Prison Rules.

Chapter 1.
Pre Prison Service.

I'll keep chapter 1 brief for this book.

I remember it like it was yesterday.
I left school in May of 1982, I didn't have a care in the world
at that time.
None of the teachers that taught me at Perth Grammar School
would believe that I ended up in the job I did.
I had no interest in education whatsoever. I got the belt or the
chalk duster thrown at me almost daily with my old
schoolmate Lee.

Employment was fairly easy to come by at that time. Not like
you could leave one job and walk straight into another but a lot
easier than it is now.
I got a job straight away in an Egg grading factory on Strathtay
road in Perth,Scotland.
Not the best of jobs but £29 in your hand at that age was a lot.

The place stank to high heaven ,as when the lorries arrived with eggs to be graded they always contained batches that had gone rotten. More often than not there were rats in the back of the lorries. I remember the driver, a stocky Irishman physically booting the rats out of his lorry, sometimes they'd splatter on the ground below. He'd boot them with some force. Apologies to rat lovers but these were massive and not your standard pet rats.

The eggs that had gone bad were green with maggots crawling in them.

It wasn't all bad. We had a great source of entertainment by the name of Norrie.

Norrie had a thick Inverness accent. All day long he would shout "Laaaaaaa" really loudly. If he was angry he'd punch boxes of eggs causing the yolk to go everywhere. But his humour was amazing.

I was only there a couple of months as it was to cover the summer period.

I didn't stay out of work for long. I saw an advert for a Hairdresser. For a laugh between my mates and I , I applied.

Lo and behold I got an interview and got the job.

Me, a hairdresser? No one would have believed it.

I was always a smart dresser due to being heavily involved in the Mod Culture.

A culture which has never left me, even to this day.

I was a massive fan of "The Jam."

I got to see them live 3 times until the bands demise in 1982.

I was devastated when they split.

A massive fan of Paul Wellers music.

Most of my late teens to early twenties I spent riding about and going to scooter rallies.

I loved the Mod Scene.

Throughout periods of my life I've had Vespas and Lambrettas.

I still dress like a Mod now.

My wardrobe heaves with Mod clothing.

The owner of the salon said that my style of dress reminded him of his style in the 1960s so it was probably that that had swayed him in my interview.

So in September 1982 I started my career as an apprentice hairdresser.

Sweeping floors, observing, inhaling the smell of perm lotion to the point where I became immune to it.

It was a great place to work. The owner was in the magic circle so there were always tricks to be watched. He once took one of my cigarettes, put it in this contraption and I thought he'd cut my fag in half. I was gutted. Cigarettes weren't cheap, even back then. Then lo and behold, he handed me my cigarette back whole. I was amazed by some of the magic he produced.

He was also a comedian so the jokes came thick and fast.

I learned my trade there.

3 Leonard Street, Perth. Now a Chinese chip shop/ restaurant.

Ian Dougall, you were always a star.

Ian used to take great delight watching my tempers when my Vespa scooter failed to start and would make hairdryer jokes about it.

A particularly funny moment in that job was a guy came came in to get his haircut. I asked him how he was doing.

" Not a great week, my dog died"

I told him I was sorry to hear this news.

He then said" My cat died as well"

I thought how unlucky he was. A cat and a dog passed in one week.
Then in the next breath he said "Oh aye, and my wife died yesterday"
I was speechless. Totally gobsmacked.
The dog, the cat and the wife in that order.

My upbringing was a great one apart from being shunted about as my father was a soldier.
Leigh on Sea , Bunde in Germany, Lisburn, Northern Ireland, Catterick, phew, I went from school to school.

In 1977 my Dad joined the Scottish Prison Service. Probably the catalyst for me in the future years.
We moved to Perth, Scotland.
I never saw much of my Dad as he worked different shifts but we did have quality time where we would go places as a family with my mother and sister Juliet.

We knew dads job was hard.
Dad worked at Perth prison back then.
The Scottish Prisons we're starting to become powderkegs and Dad would play an intrinsic part in the following years.

In the 80s Scottish Prisons erupted.
The worst was the Peterhead disturbances.
Dad was sent there as part of the Riot team. When they all mustered it was noticeable they had no hostage negotiator.
Bearing in mind they had an Officer hostage on the roof.
A prison psychologist who knew my dad said "Les is the man to do this"
 Dad had never negotiated before but his way of dealing with things calmly and professionally put him right on the frontline

facing some of the most dangerous, hardened prisoners in Scotland.

Dad negotiated from below the roofs skylight. He had a helmet as protection and that was it.
One of the Prisoners was dousing my dad with lighter fluid.
Dad did not budge, he stood like a rock despite the threats to set him alight.
Eventually it got to crisis point and the SAS were sent in to quell the disturbance.
Dad attended a lot of sieges in his time.

My Dad stayed a negotiator until my mum Lynda said enough was enough
Dad was our rock and he is sadly missed by us all but his legacy during that riot lives on.
Les Duncan, you were a legend as a Dad and a Prison Officer.

My Father passed away in February 2022.
A massive loss.

I cracked on in my hairdressing and began renting a chair in 1985 in Ian's salon.
I was drawing in good business and once Ian showed me the figures of my takings per week it was a no brainier.
Renting a chair was a great idea.
Business was booming but I wanted something more.
Self employment and having young family wasn't great. Time off was lost money.
I was eager to do something with more grit about it.
I was married and my 1st born Jay was only a toddler. He was born in 1993.

In 1994 I applied to the Scottish Prison Service and passed. At the same time though I'd applied to Prisons in England. HMP Whitemoor had invited me for assessment and an interview.

At that time the Scottish Prison Service we're paying £12,500 a year.

Down south it was £15,700.

I swithered and then opted for Whitemoor.

The assessment test was the same as the SPS so I'd already done it previously. Needless to say, I passed.

Next step was the interview.

Mine was in a place called March in Cambridgeshire.

I got my Interview roughly an hour after the test. There were quite a few of us waiting anxiously to face the interview panel.

My turn came.

I walked into the room.

3 on the panel, and a chair which sat away from the panels desk.

Akin to a game show contestant.

I got asked a series of questions eg .. What would you do if?..,, What experiences /qualities can you bring to the Prison Service?....

I answered to the best of my ability.

I had been a Special Constable in Perth for 3 years prior so I could relate to a lot of the questions.

After the interview I took the long train ride back to Perth. The interview was a Wednesday. It was a waiting game.

I came home from work on the Friday that week. The house phone was flashing stating I had a message.

I pressed the button to hear it.

The message said "Hi, this is John Pryme from HMP Whitemoor, congratulations, you've got the job"
I was absolutely ecstatic.
I was a Prison Officer.
My dads influence must have been there somewhere.

Chapter 2

The beginning.

This was it. I got the job with grit that I was looking for. I'd spent years standing behind a chair talking to a mirror. The usual "Where you going on holiday?"
"What you up to today?" And so on..
I met and became friends with so many people working in that hairdressers.

I got my joining date of February 1995.
I remember telling Ian ,who owned the salon that I was leaving. I was choked, holding back tears as I'd spent 12 years there. Ian and Pam were so good to me during my time there. I can't thank them enough.

So the day came to start training. I'd sorted out accommodation in a lovely old cottage next to the River Nene in March town centre. Lizzie who owned the cottage reminded me of an ageing hippie. She had this quaint cottage coloured pink on the outside. 2 doors down was a lovely public house as well.

Day 1 was a tour of Whitemoor. I didn't know much about the jail itself apart from the escape from the Special Secure Unit (SSU) a couple of years prior. Whitemoor is a Category A max

security Prison. It houses the worst criminals in England.
Serial killers, murderers, terrorists, child killers.
Lovely eh?
From pleasantly cutting hair to this.

Week one was a lot of touring of the Jail.
Surprisingly I didn't find it as daunting as I thought it would
be.
Mind you it wasn't an old Victorian jail. Quite freshly painted,
in cell toilets , all single occupancy cells, tv rooms, kitchens on
each spur.
A spur is made up of 3 landings. The ones, the twos and the
threes landings as they were called.
Each wing had 3 spurs coming off the centre. So in total each
wing had nine landings.
Red spur, Blue Spur and Green spur.
90 Prisoners to a spur.

The centre office was located on the twos landing.
I'd never seen so many gates and doors in one place in my life.
Constant clanging and banging.

During week 1 as expected, a lot of the Prisoners spoke, a lot
gave you the stare to try and put you off.
I wasn't phased by it whatsoever.
Mind you, there was some fucking big lumps in there. Guys
you wouldn't like to bump into in a dark alley.
The staff I met were great. None tried to put us off at all. Very
welcoming.
I knew enough from my Dad about prisons so I kind of knew
what I was letting myself in for.

Week 2 was College time. A time I'll never forget.

Joining us on our 9 weeks training were 4 staff from Everthorpe prison near Hull and Sharpie from daaan Saaath or down South translated.

45 of us put into a 4 star hotel in a little town called Daventry.

We were put n the Brittania Hotel.

No longer standing now.

Developers must have got in there with a good offer.

The college accommodation at Newbold Revel near Rugby was undergoing refurbishment so they put us in the hotel.

What were they thinking?

45 people on a course in a 4 star hotel.

Madness .

The Brittania was quite a big hotel akin to Hotel chains now and the rooms were quite pleasant.

Some of us had travelled by train to get to Daventry from March on the Sunday afternoon.

We were armed with our Alcohol carry outs and had some great laughs on the journey. Sort of Bonding with beer.

By the time we got to the hotel we were half cut.

If memory serves me well there were 8 of us on that train .

We arranged to meet at the bar, joined by others who had travelled by car, other trains etc… in the end the whole course was at the bar. All 45. Some of us had a head start with the alcohol.

Monday morning.

Day 1.

Newbold Revel.

I woke up at 6.30am rough as fuck. Knowing I was facing breakfast which was buffet style eat all you want.

I needed it.

We had a 30 minute coach ride to the college ahead of us. I managed breakfast after ironing my uniform.
I could see that I wasn't the only one that was rough as a badgers arse.
I must've downed nearly a full jug of orange juice in that sitting. The juice jugs were getting topped up every 60 seconds I reckon. 40 odd rough new Prison Officers. " The Naughty Forty" as we became known.
We hadn't even got to college and felt like we'd done 2 days work.

Getting on that coach you could smell the alcohol .
A match light would've set the bus up.
That was the first of many rough journeys.

Mark H was the comedian though and had us laughing on most journeys.
He was loud and funny.
There was Mark H, Sharpie, Terry, myself and a few others all had the same sick sense of humour so we got on great.
It broke up the monotony of the journey daily. It really was a Bastard of a journey every day.
That poor coach driver.
I reckon he'd have failed the breathalyser from our alcohol fumes .

Newbold Revel was an old mansion styled building . Quite grand in its day I can imagine. Big brown building.
I remember going through them barriers for the very first time that Monday morning. Facing the big old building that was to be our training area for 9 weeks, Monday to Friday.
We all piled into the reception area to collect ID and bits to be then taken to a fairly big classroom.

I sat next to Sharpie the Southern geezer. Sharpie was about 6ft 4 and resembled Reg Kray facially so immediately he got the name Reggie.

He drove a big old 50s American gas guzzler.

We had bonded straight away. He was a brilliant artist and drew caricatures of us all.

In came our tutors to introduce themselves. Principal Officer Harry Dixon, a smallish spectacled bloke with a north east accent and senior Officer Richard Jordan. Stocky ish bloke with a very midlands accent.

They introduced themselves and then made us do the Creeping Death, where individually you stand up and introduce yourself over a period of 3 minutes telling your colleagues about your life, likes and dislikes.

Kev in our class said "I dislike the IRA" Irish Republican Army.

Ironic,as Kev , like myself would go onto a landing where the IRA were housed.

Harry Dixon in his geordie accent said
"Yous are all Prison Officers now and your conduct has to be exemplary"

I thought back to the rowdiness the night before and thought "Exemplary."Fuck.

That first night would come back and haunt us all.

We had a tour of the whole of Newbold Revel the first day. The area was a lot bigger than I thought. Football and rugby pitches, a gym, study areas and a bar.

The bar was cheaper than the hotel but we were stuck in Daventry.

Imprisoned in the Brittania . Until we discovered the bars in Daventry.

We got on well with the locals we met there. We frequented a few local pubs.
There was a local called "Frog"who set up football matches against the locals on an Astro turf pitch which was great fun.

On one occasion we were walking back to the hotel. One girl on the course Miranda was walking along chatting. Next thing she was gone.
All we heard was a screamy type squeak for help. She'd fallen down an uncovered manhole.
Miranda had bruising and grazes but recovered.

Night 2 at the Brittania carried on as night one had left off. Noisy, rowdy and out of hand. I'm not going to lie, our conduct was not what Harry Dixon would have called " Exemplary".

Day 2 at Newbold and word had got back from Hotel management to our HR which in turn got back to our respective Prisons.
Harry Dixon told us to expect a visit from management.

Our classes were a lot of Death by PowerPoint . Most of us had the droopy eye syndrome . But we did get practical exercises. The first one was using radio communication inside prisons. They had us using the phonetic alphabet.
Kev was ex Royal Navy and was based onshore throughout his career.
Harry Dixon called to Kevs callsign.

"Using phonetic alphabet , tell me the name of the last ship you served on?"

We all burst as Kev replied in his soft Dumfriesshire accent.
" I've never served on a ship"

There were 3 of us on that course from Scotland. Kev, Alan and myself. I found out Kev was travelling home to Aberdeen every Friday so we car shared from then on.

On night 3 at Daventry I had a conversation with one of the guys on the course called Barry, a scouser.
He asked where I was from.
I told him.

He said his daughter lived there and was a Hairdresser. Turns out I worked with Emma, his daughter in the same salon.
Small world.
That same night I bumped into someone else I knew from Perth.

Day 4 at Newbold we got roasted.
Managers at Whitemoor appeared in our class and we were warned that if there were any more Hotel complaints we would be all out of a job.
We had to screw the nut.

So we were on 9 weeks of Prison Officer training. We were known as NEPOs
New Entrant Prison Officers.
We had to learn every aspect of the job.
From how to be nice to control and restraint (C and R)when things go bad.

C and R was fun. It started of nice and gentle then full on with us donning helmets and protective padding.

We'd take turns at being Prisoners resisting and the other colleagues had to restrain you.

It did get quite heavy going at times rolling about on the mats in the DOJO.

I'd later on in my career be donning the helmet rather a lot as I joined the Prison Service riot team.

A lot of the training was focused on interpersonal skills and conflict management. This was an essential part of the job. They did Drug awareness where they lit a bong with solid cannabis.

It got passed to Sharpie and me. After we'd had a go there wasn't much left of it.

We got the giggles which then reverberated round the classroom.

Searching was a thing I enjoyed . They had a mock cell at Newbold and they'd hide things in it.

I was adept at this.

I ended up teaching Searching techniques to Prison staff later on and made an appearance on the BBC showing weapons.

Harry Dixon and Richard Jordan were brilliant tutors. Harry told prison stories and anecdotes a lot. Ones he kept repeating.

I remember him describing one prisoner as a " Hard hitter"

" If he hit you you'd think there was a crowd round you" he'd say on more than one occasion.

The prisoner he described would be one on my wing.

A chap called "Burkett."

We got to our 2nd last evening of college and had set up a party of which surprisingly the Hotel let us host.

What a night. What a laugh. Party games, music and some Officers from Whitemoor had turned up too.

I'll never forget Wolfy from Everthorpe , a jail near Hull doing his Whigfield "Saturday night "dance routine. It was bang on perfect.

The tune at the time was "Back for good" by Take that.

That was the last tune played at that party. Every time I hear that track it takes me back.

The day came when we graduated. All 45 remained.

No drop outs which shocked me a bit. There's usually one or two but we'd all kept each other going. There were even times when I thought about packing in and going home but all in all a real Team effort.

Our families were there to see us proudly pass out.

During the ceremony, my then 2 year old son saw me just as our Governor Brodie Clark started his speech.

Jay shouted " That's my Dad"

To which Brodie said

" Contrary to what the little boy says, I'm not his father"

A real funny moment.

We received our certificates from Brodie and training was over.

We said our goodbyes to colleagues who were going to work at other jails.

Sharpie , on saying goodbye burst into tears.

It was a poignant moment as we had all bonded so well over the weeks.

It was the real thing now.

Not training.

This was it.

Here we go. C-Wing.

It was a warm sunny Monday morning the next time all 40 of us met again in the staff mess at Whitemoor.
40 crisp White shirts sat eagerly awaiting word of where we were working.
Finally we all had our placements.

I got C Wing which housed the likes of IRA Terrorists, murderers, big drug dealers , armed robbers, Gangsters etc..
I was delighted with that.
I'd been round C wing during our tour weeks before.
The Wing Governor was a lovely bloke called Tom Naughton who stayed in the digs that I was staying in.
I drew my keys and went to C Wing.

On arrival there were 4 of us from the course placed there.
Tom, Alan, Miranda and myself.
We were met by the Wing Senior Officer in the briefing room.
Dave welcomed us to the wing and then took us around the 3 Spurs of the wing.
Blue spur was blocked off from the other Spurs as it was classed as an enhanced unit for prisoners who had good conduct.
It had a range of activities for the Prisoners housed there, including its own gym.
After the tour we were placed on spurs to work.
I got Red spur and was introduced to Mark who I would shadow whilst on duty.
Mark was a local lad who had 2 years as an Officer.
He talked me through the core day and how the wing ran.
One member of staff said

"Forget everything you learned at College"

The main feeding area was known as the servery or hot plate.
There was a cleaning officer who supervised the servery area
with 2 orderlies who were trusted prisoners.
Well, trusted enough to serve food.
The food left a lot to be desired but if memory serves me well
it cost under £2 to feed each prisoner per day at that time.
You wouldn't believe this but on day 1 of me being on the
wing during serving, a used condom floated to the top of the
custard. We saw it was used as it was tied up at the top and
there was definetly some kind of stuff inside it resembling
semen.
At a later date faeces was found on C wing in the gravy.
The food was prepared in a main kitchen, brought to the wing
via an orderly and served. The prisoners in the kitchen had all
the time in the world to put anything inside the food tins and
tubs.
In the mornings a lot of the prisoners went to work in the
various workshops that there were at Whitemoor.
Joinery, industrial cleaning , education , gym etc..
These were the places that prisoners from other wings mixed.
That wasn't always a good thing.

I'd been at Whitemoor for under 2 weeks.
I escorted a High Risk Category A prisoner to the gym after
workshop movement was completed.
There are 3 types of category A prisoners.
Exceptional Risk Cat A.
High Risk Cat A.
Standard risk cat A.
These categories take into consideration. Escape risk, resources
to aiding escape by outsiders and risk to the public.

When you move an exceptional risk or a high risk cat A you escort them one on one or two officers on one dependent on the individual. You take a book with you with timings of movement. It's a small blue book with their prison number, wing and a photo. Kind of like a passport.

You sign to say you have the prisoner and what time you left the wing with him. When you reach your destination the officer of that destination signs when he receives the prisoner to his custody.

For example Visits, Gym, workshops etc…

On visits, Exceptional Risk and High Risk cat A's have a room dedicated to this.

They don't get into the main visits hall.

Exceptional risk prisoners are housed in a Special Secure Unit (SSU) but we will go into that later.

I got to the gym via the long corridor from C wing chatting with the prisoner who to be honest was quite a pleasant guy to deal with,passing the entrances to A and B wing.

A and B were wings housing VPs (Vulnerable Prisoners)

Sex offenders and debtors. Basically anyone who could not be housed on C and D wings.

I handed my prisoner over to the gym officer known as (PEO).

Physical Education officers. They are prison officers who specialise in physical education.

I turned to walk back to C wing.

Just as I did that I heard an almighty scream and a clang. I turned.

A prisoner had been bench pressing.

As he put his weights back ,another prisoner smacked him on the head with a dumbbell.

Now, I've seen blood but never like this.

I saw the white of his skull very briefly before a waterfall of red ran down his face. His whole body was soaked in blood.He tried to get up but fell back on the weights bench. I hit the alarm bell.

Quickly the cavalry arrived. About 20 officers got to the scene very quickly including medical staff.

The assailant was restrained using C and R methods and taken away.

It was carnage. The gym floor was a sea of red.

It wasn't long before an ambulance arrived.

The prisoner was on my wing, as was the assailant.

I never saw him again,but we were informed that he had suffered brain damage so severe that he couldn't talk or walk after that. He was very lucky to survive this horrific attack. I'll never forget the scream though. When I think of it , I can still hear it.

I'd settled into working on C wing.

I was popular on a dinner time with all grades of the jail from Governors down to Officers ringing to see if I was on duty and could I cut their hair on my dinner break. It was handy being an ex hairdresser.

I started to notice that there was an atmosphere on the landings. An eerie feeling.

I put in Security information reports (SIRs) stating what I'd seen and heard. Any observations that were out of the ordinary. Usually Prisoners who normally chat with you that stop engaging.

I knew something was wrong.

Staff didn't really believe me at the time. I was a newbie.

A couple of days after submitting this, C wing prisoners staged a sit out.

They broke cell door handles and sat on the landings refusing to bang up despite the wing Governor giving them a direct order to return to their cells.

This was a peaceful protest.

Eventually around 11pm at night,they all banged up without any damage bar the door handles.

I got the task of having to write a nicking sheet for each individual prisoner for refusing a direct order to return to cell.

This is called placing a prisoner on report.

With this they face the Governor, kind of an in prison court. They can be given certain punishments. Loss of canteen, loss of earnings, cellular confinement etc..

I had to hand write 80 odd nicking sheets and get them processed in time to be presented as evidence to the Governor. It took me bloody ages.

I felt something else would follow from this protest.

I was right.

After the protest the wing seemed peaceful enough Day to day it was going smoothly , or so I thought until one day I was coming out of a workshop.

I heard a prisoner say to another one

" Don't talk to the screws, blank them"

The prisoner that said this normally got on with staff without any issues.

I knew something was wrong. Gut instinct tells you. You can feel the tension.

Again I submitted SIRs to security.

Again they were basically laughed off.

C-wing Riot.

2 days later I was on Red spur with Ian, an Officer I got on brilliantly with and am still in contact with now. I think the other Officer on Red spur was Steve.

Prisoners we're beginning to gather, the atmosphere was unreal, it's hard to describe in words.

I was patrolling the 2s landing but a prisoner said
" There's a fire in the TV room".

Immediately I went onto the ones landing where I saw smoke bellowing from the room. By this time , unbeknown to me , Prisoners had broken Pencils in the locks so I had only one route off Red spur.

The ones landing gate.

I looked up, there was no way off. All routes were blocked. I was trapped and had prisoners coming towards me. 2 actually got a hold of me.

By this time some of them were starting to smash furniture and the music got louder .

Blaring Queens hit " We will Rock you"

I looked around and up. Above me some prisoners were dangling a metal bed.

One Prisoner shouted
" you're gonna die today Mr Duncan"

They were going to drop it and it was right above me,had it dropped would've easily broken my neck.

I'm not joking when I say my life flashed before me.

I'm either going to die or be taken hostage.

Now some prisoners hated Prison Officers, others saw us as guys just doing a job.

Luckily a very influential Prisoner nicknamed "Bullet" stepped in and bellowed across the spur.

" Your fight is with the system, not Mr Duncan"

He took me to the ones gate and I unlocked it and got off the spur.

As soon as I got off the spur stuff started flying toward me. Jars of faeces included,but I was safe ish at least.
I looked across to see Green spur was the same. Blue spur had all banged up not wanting to get involved.
The noise was deafening as they ran around tearing up the spurs. Furniture, pool tables, table tennis tables. Basically anything that they could trash, they trashed it.
There was smoke and water everywhere.
It was chaos.

I managed to get up to the centre office.
I was visibly shaken as anyone would be. The senior Officer that day asked me if I was ok and sent me to the briefing room where other staff were.
We were all shaken up.
If it wasn't for a Prisoner, god knows what would have happened to me.
It still traumatises me now when I think about it.

The riot team were called in. Known as MUFTI at that time. " Minimum use of Force and Tactical Unit"
Within a couple hours the wing was taken back.
MUFTI we're ruthless in taking back C Wing.
Some prisoners surrendered as soon as the teams entered the spurs. One prisoner pissed himself and messed his pants, it was visible through his light grey track suit bottoms. Standard issue for prisoners.
The noise was even more deafening once the teams came on.
Prisoners we're scattering like mice into mouse holes. Some tried to fight against the Perspex shields but it was in vain.
There were prisoners lined up all along the spurs after that.

The main perpetrators taken in locks and handcuffs down to the segregation unit.

I'd have been scared facing the teams . Imagine the hoard of blue overalls, helmets and shields coming at you all gagging for action.

To be honest , it was a great display to watch.

A display I would join at a later date.

We found out that C and D wings had got their days mixed up or there would have been rioting on both wings that day.

I found out later that the reason for the riot was that a High Risk prisoner got a smaller piece of chicken at the servery than a Category B prisoner .

It's the small things that matter eh?

Calm after the storm. (Kind of)

After the riot that day the wing went quiet for some time.

We had alarm bells , mostly false. Pressed to see staff reaction times in a lot of cases to see how many officers would respond.

Believe me, it sounded like a herd of elephants running up the corridor when alarm bells rang on the wings.

Now, talking of Elephants, here's a story that has probably been talked of many a time. I know I still get ribbed about it.

I was designated as a yards party officer.

The yard party consisted of 4 prisoners and me.

One freezing cold December we went out to pick up wheelie bins to take to the bin compound.

Off we went from the wing outside to the side of C and D wings to collect said bins.

They were padlocked up.

Also, they were iced up.

Could I unlock the padlock? Not a chance.

The prisoners on my party found it amusing.

I however got frustrated and a bit angry.

The prisoners started making noises at me as I battled to get a key into said padlock.

I had to take them back to the wing as we couldn't get the bins out.

All the way back to the wing they kept making noises.

I decided to place them all on report for a Disrespects any Officer charge.

The adjudication for this began in the office in the segregation unit.

My charge sheet basically said

"Placed on report for making animal noises whilst carrying out my duties as a yards party officer"

Well, during this, one prisoner said

" I'd like to ask Mr Duncan what noise we made"

I thought , oh no, this will end up making me look like an idiot.

So without physically making the noise I replied

" Elephant noises Governor"

Well, the Seg staff, the Governor and the prisoner all burst out laughing spontaneously.

The charge was dropped.

I returned from the seg to c wing.

I was welcomed back to the sound of the whole wing making elephant noises.

2 days later I received an internal mail.

Enclosed was an elephant mask , the kind from a game where someone wears it and others try and throw hoops onto its trunk.

Thank you Visits Senior Officer Colin for that lovely gift.

I got phone calls from other wings asking if Nellie was on duty or they'd make elephant sounds or say "Hi, this is a trunk call".

I remember my first week as a yards officer. I still chuckle at thinking about this one.
I came on duty one morning. The Senior Officer said
" Tony, can you take one prisoner to reception?"
I said
Yes, remember I've got yards party to do"
He said no problem. I toddled off to reception with said Prisoner.
I returned to the wing.
The senior officer then asked if I could take one to Education.
I told him I had yards party to take out.
He replied,
" That's ok, take them out when you come back"
I said ok and went to Education with another prisoner.
When I got back the same SO came up to me and said
" I've had the control room onto me, why aren't the yards party out?"
I replied "probably because I can't be in 3 bloody places at once"

Ian, one of my colleagues once ordered another Officer a stannah Stairlift trial.
There was some humour on the wings between staff.
Ian got my jersey out of the briefing room, ran it under a tap, folded it up and put it in the freezer. Thus ruining said jersey.
In retaliation , I got his lunchbox, opened up his sandwiches and sprinkled boot polish in them. All fun. Probably classed as bullying now.

I started this chapter as the Calm after the storm.

Yes it was , until one day on red spur there was an almighty bang.

Turns out the INLA and IRA prisoners had built a bomb using powdered milk to help it go off. It was inside a plastic dustbin on Red spur. It was some bang. The dustbin was completely melted.

Then.

Probably the worst day in Whitemoors history.

It was a Sunday afternoon.

Prisoners did their usual.

Cooking.

The kitchen on red spur was always busy on a Sunday.

Prisoners clubbed together to buy food. The ones with money ate better than I did. Big roasts with all the trimmings.

I found this disgusting to be honest.

Them eating like kings and I shopped in Aldi or Lidl.

Mid afternoon a prisoner reported that another prisoner was cooking a lot of hot oil.

The prisoner was told that there was no limit on oil.

He did say that he thought the oil was going to be used on someone.

He was told to go away and stop bothering people.

Shortly afterwards the alarm bell was pressed by a prisoner.

Staff responded and ran from the threes landing to the twos landing.

The alarm bell was a set up.

One of my colleagues was first to the twos only to be confronted by a prisoner holding 2 jugs of boiling hot fat.

The prisoner then threw both jugfuls of fat straight at him.
Immediately my colleagues skin started to bubble. It had been
thrown at his face and torso.
Prisoners , on seeing this got hold of my colleague and rushed
him to the shower room.
Even they were horrified at this.
They got him under the shower and were running a cold bath
to try and help.
They could've taken his keys but no.
They had wedged a phone card into the shower button to
enable it to keep running as it only ran for a short period of
time before cutting out. Very quick thinking.
It shows that even prisoners have compassion.
The assailant, in fear of his life from other prisoners had ran
like a coward to his cell.
I heard other prisoners say they were going to do him in for his
actions.

I went to visit my colleague at Leicester burns unit a few days
later with another colleague Scott.
We both left in tears. I mean floods of tears.
His burns were horrific.
My colleague came back after a few months to thank the
prisoners who had helped him.
That was the most poignant moment I've ever seen.
It upset a lot of prisoners seeing him the way that it had
affected him.
Some were in tears.
That was his last time at Whitemoor.

A few years later my colleague took his own life.
A dark dark time.

Days after that incident 3 of us were stood on the 3's landing.

A Principal Officer came onto the spur.
He said to me "Which Landing are you on ?"
I told him the threes landing.
He turned to the other 2 staff, Ian being one of them and told
them to go to their landings.
I immediately said
"Safety in numbers, we're staying here"
He scowled at me and said
" I'm 2 ranks above you"
I replied
" yeah and me and my 2 colleagues here want to go home
without injury tonight"

He stormed off disgruntled.

Now one particularly bad side of the Prison Service is " bent
screws".
Whitemoor had them,as did every jail.
A few rotten apples in a barrel as they say.
A few female staff had been caught having inappropriate
relationships with prisoners. A few made the National press.
I couldn't get my head around it.
Why join a job with decent money and risk it?
It's not like a relationship with a life sentenced prisoner is
going anywhere. Desperate if you ask me.

Did C wing have one?
Yes we did and it affected me directly.
Bearing in mind here we housed Terrorists, killers and hitmen
on the wing. People with outside connections.
Earlier I mentioned that I was a yards party officer.
There was a prisoner on that party I did not get on with.
He came to me on the yards party one morning and handed me
a piece of folded paper.

I opened it up.

Written on the piece of paper was my address, car make and colour, car reg plate and what school my son went to.

I couldn't believe what I was reading.

"Where did you get this?" I asked.

The prisoner replied with

" You can't trust everyone Mr Duncan" and laughed.

Immediately I took the yards party back onto the wing.

I went straight to my wing manager and showed him the piece of paper.

Immediately plans were put in place to move the prisoner.

My thought was who else had this piece of paper with my personal details on it? IRA?, Gangsters?

anyone on that wing could've passed my details on.

The prisoner was moved to D wing.

I thought he should have been moved out of the prison.

2 days later I got into my car and drove from the little Fenland village where I lived.

Now, no one came to Wimblington village unless they had family there.

It had one shop, 1 pub and a school.

That was it.

There was a white sports car sitting along from my house with its engine running.

Going to work you wouldn't have known I was a Prison Officer.

I got changed in the facilities building at work. I had jeans on and a khaki green MA1 flight jacket on,adorned with Scooter club patches.

I drove out of the street as did the white sports car.

Never gave it much thought at the time. I got to the roundabout at the end of the village and got onto the long straight road into March Town itself.

The white car still behind me. It got closer and closer almost bumper to bumper.

The car then overtook me.

I looked over.

There was one guy in the car who then made his fingers look like a pistol aiming at me.

He sped off.

Luckily I got the reg number. I wrote it on a piece of paper, a receipt I think.

I did write the Reg exact.

I drove straight into March police station explaining what had happened.

They took all details and told me to go and see the prisons Police liaison Officer. PLOs are police officers that work within a jail closely with the security department.

I got to work and immediately went to see the PLO.

" There's no car registered with that plate Tony" he told me.

I knew I was being targeted from then on in.

Next bit was even more convincing.

I had to pop to D wing.

On there was the prisoner who had passed me the piece of paper days before.

" How did you get to work this morning Mr Duncan? I thought you'd have been run off the road"

That was it. The White sports car.

It had been a set up, a scare, a warning.

Where the hell had all this info come from?

Meanwhile , an officer who I worked with had been caught at the local post office by the CID.

He was on holiday in Jamaica. During the holiday he had done some kind of deal whilst there.

When the package arrived it had split and the cannabis inside it became visible.

Now this Officer I would not have expected of wrongdoings.

He seemed to me a firm but fair Officer who took no nonsense.

It never dawned on me at first ,but if you were on nights it was a bonus if he was on an early start.

Nights finished at 07.30 as a rule but if someone came in early and did the roll count you were gone, shift over.

This Officer would appear on the wing just after 06.30 thus you'd be away around 06.45.

No wonder he was in early.

Turns out he was distributing drugs under cell doors once you had left the wing.

He ended up on remand at HMP Norwich.

During his remand he asked for a Governor to visit him to give him some information.

The info was relating to him being involved in an escape attempt at the Prison.

He was going to pretend he was a hostage whilst some prisoners made their escape via helicopter.

The named Prisoners were put in the SSU as exceptional risk Cat As.

All denied their part in an escape plot.

When working on Wings you notice who has clout.

This was noticeable when C and D wing played each other on the Astro turf pitch on a weekend.

There was a certain London Gangster, who every weekend would get a deciding penalty.

Now I know C Wings keeper could comfortably save the penalty, you could wager he could save it, but every week the London lad scored.

We used to say to C Wings keeper

" You could've saved that"

He'd reply

" I know but I prefer my arms and legs unbroken"

Not that you get along with every Prisoner.

There was one that I kind of locked horns with.

He was a South London gangster called Downer. He was related , and a co defendent of the penalty scoring London Gangster mentioned earlier.

He strutted about the landings ,arms out like he had a roll of carpet under each arm.

The hard man swagger.

Liam Gallagher of Oasis would've stood in awe at this swagger.

Downer used to boast

"I ain't lost a fight since 1958"

I nicked Downer for wiring up to his light system. Wiring up is dangerous.

They take electrical wire, attach it to a radio, burn a hole in their strip light in the cell, attach it to the electrics system in the light so it saves on radio batteries which they have to purchase from the canteen. Thus saving money.

From that day on Downer waged a war we me as sorts.

Each time he tried something I nicked him.

I remember one day he shouted across green spur loudly.

" No one speak to Mr Duncan he's a horrible muggy cunt"

He tried to turn the whole wing against me all over a nicking.
The majority of Prisoners took a nicking and forgot about it
straight away. Not Downer.
He couldn't accept he'd been caught out.
His winning everything since 1958 had come to an end.

His penultimate nicking was in visits.
I was patrolling the visits hall and walked past him. He had
young children on the visit. He stood up and got really verbal
and loud.
" You're a fuckin arsewipe Duncan, I'll do you"
All in front of visitors including children.
He came right up to me in my face. Fists ready to punch.
I had no choice I had to jump him.
I got him onto the floor and other staff arrived. We restrained
him and took him straight out of the visits hall.
I mean there's a time and a place ,and in front of the public is
not the place.

Visits is a good thing for prisoners. They get to see family and
friends.
Something they look forward to, a sense of normality. You
have to remember that they have lost their liberty and it is their
only contact with the outside world.
So to behave in this manner on a visit is nothing short of
deplorable.
You could see his visitors visibly shaken. The children
especially.

After a few months Downer asked to speak to me privately in
an office.
He apologised for all the hassle, shook my hand and his war
ended with me.

Not the only person to wager war with me. There were a few ,
but one bad one was a Philippino Prisoner.
This guy had previously sharpened toilet brushes.
Now they are deadly.
Hard plastic ,sharpened to a point.
Scary weapons.

I nicked him for disrespect.
He decided to get his own back on me.
I was doing locks, bolts and bars. (LBBs)
The prisoner had clocked me doing this.
I remember it was absolutely roasting that day.
During LBBs you check doors, fittings, bars etc.. in the cells.
On knowing we tap the bars to check for any tampering, the
prisoner smeared jam on the outside of the bars.
When I tapped them ,around 30 wasps flew straight into the
cell.
He'd done it deliberately so I'd get stung.
Luckily I didn't.

The same prisoner fell out with Gary on my wing so wired his
light to the bars.
When Gary tapped his bars he got thrown to the other side of
the cell with electric shock. He also had a black burn on his
hand from it.
Wiring up was a big danger to us.

I recall another bad incident involving a prisoner and a
Governor.
The prisoner was a non conformist totally. He'd do anything to
fight the system. He never spoke to prisoners much, never
mind staff. The prisoner was a martial arts expert as well so he
was always well watched by staff.

The prisoner was taken to a wing office to speak with the head of residential who was a Governor 4.

There were 5 tiers of Governor.

The number 1 Governor, who is the Governing Governor down to Governor 5.

There was Governors of the works Department and Wing Governors and so on..

Anyway, this prisoner was sat down not really listening, just playing with his fingers. There were 3 of us in the office in case the prisoner kicked off. He had a reputation for it.

Suddenly, he forked his fingers and quick as a flash he put his fingers into the Governors eyes.

Immediately we floored the prisoner and in wrist locks we took him to the segregation unit.

The head of residential could easily have been blinded with the speed and force used.

C Wing had some characters both staff and prisoner.

A particular prisoner stood out. He never mixed with others and always seemed a bit odd.

One morning I was in the workshop and noticed he kept going into the cleaning cupboard. I decided to follow him.

To my surprise I found him eating handfuls of Swarfega, which for those that don't know ,it's a green petroleum based cleaner.

I know the prison food wasn't great , but really!!!!

Another prisoner told me of his robbery on a mobile cash van.
Bigging himself up
to be a big heist guy.

I never really read prisoners records unless it was to do a report on them so I didn't know his case details.

A programme came on TV one night and there he was.

Him and his co defendants had indeed got into a mobile cash van but the raid bungled and every single note of it caught fire.
I was on duty the next day. I saw him cleaning the landing on green spur.
" Money to burn have you?" I laughed.
He muttered and went red faced.

Another Prisoner used to sit with a plastic bag on the top of his head and said it was because steam came out of his head.
Strange.

Earlier on I mentioned a Prisoner my training PO spoke of a lot.
" Burkett"
Well this guy might have been a hard hitter as Harry Dixon had told us but Burkett also had a photographic memory.
He came to the Centre office one day and handed an officer a plastic knife. Prisoners used plastic cutlery.
The said knife was shaped into a key.
It had been made so well that it opened the spur gates.
Can you imagine what could happen if 270 prisoners got off theirs spurs.
There was less than 20 staff on the wing.
The odds aren't great if it goes Pear shaped.
Burkett as a rule was no problem. Very old school.
But his potential was a huge problem.

One thing I should mention is "Dirty Protests".
Not pleasant.
On quite a few occasions I've had to don the white paper suit and walk into a shit smeared cell, looking like a giant condom.
Usually these happen in Segregation units but I have dealt with them on wings before.
When I say it reeks, I sincerely mean that.

Especially in summertime.

They cake the excrement on themselves, walls, ceilings, occasionally they'll write messages on the wall with it.

I'm not kidding when I say you wretch when dealing with it.

I remember when Whitemoors Seg unit had a couple on the protest one summer, the stench wafted onto the wings.

It was gut wrenching, but like when I was a hairdresser I said I got used to the smell of Perm lotion, so,I got used to the smell of shit.

It's strange how you are so far away from Home and all of a sudden you're reminded of it.

I was walking down the corridor. I saw a group of new officers waiting to go on B Wing.

I got to the gate to let them in.

All I heard was

" Amazing that they let you in here Tony Duncan"

I looked up , it was George, a guy I knew years ago from Perth.

He ended up on C Wing with me.

Then not long later, me and George were on Green spur when a new officer to Whitemoor walked on.

I thought I recognised him.

He introduced himself as Barry.

I asked him where in Scotland he was from.

" I'm fae Perth" he said.

Me and George burst out laughing.

" So are we" I laughed.

I thought I recognised him.

He was a local DJ back in the fair City years ago.

3 Perth folk on one Wing, a long way from home.

We weren't the only ones.

I was on A wing covering an Evening duty.

A prisoner approached me. His first words were,
" Do you still have scooters?"
I said " What makes you think I have Scooters?"
"I remember you being a Mod in Perth" he replied.
I asked him how he knew who I was.
He told me he was in my Younger sister Juliet's class at school
and how he used to hang around my old street watching the
streams of Scooters parked outside our house.
He described my scooter and the house I lived in with my
parents years ago.
Turns out the guy was at School with my sister.
He was doing a life sentence.
He raped and killed a girl whilst he was in the Army.

Staff wise we had some laughs.

One of my colleagues was sat eating his sandwich.
A wasp flew right up to him.
It was a face off between him and little waspy.
The wasp hovered, my colleague tried to blow it away. As he
blew, the wasp flew straight into his mouth.
Luckily it never stung him but we all pissed ourselves
laughing.

There were the usual pranks by staff like blackening the
telephone with boot polish so when you answered the phone
your ear ended up black.
Sellotaping insides of doors so when you walked in you
walked straight into sellotape.
Clingfilm on toilet bowls. Jumpers in freezers to name a few.
My colleague Ian being the worst for said pranks.
Humour got us through the day.

Earlier I mentioned Helicopters. This reminds me of a wind up done on me which is also infamous at Whitemoor along with the Elephant incident.

I was told secretly that I was to be part of a covert Armed escort to take an infamous Italian Mafia hit man off our wing back to Italy.
It was helicopters, jets, flak jackets and that I had to go on a firearms course for this highest of high profile escorts.
I was over the moon to be offered this exciting opportunity.
They were telling me that there was a possibility that there would be trouble from the Mafia and attempts to free him.
Hence the firearms course.

Everyday staff would ask how I was feeling about the escort. I was buzzing to do it.
They told me that the training department were looking to put me on the firearms course within the next few days. I was so looking forward to it.

A few days passed . A colleague of mine Gary, sadly no longer with us ,said to me "Hey Tony what's that country shaped like a boot on the map?"
"Italy" I replied.
He then pointed to his nether regions and said
" What are these?"
"Bollocks" I said.
He told me to put the two words together.
Italy, bollocks.
It had been a big wind up.
I was gutted to say the least but it was entertainment for the staff seeing me buzzing at the prospect.
I hear it's a story that still goes around in the jail to this day.

Prison work wasn't all doom, gloom and violence.

We got a lot of Escorts in Cat A jails.
Prisoners tend to get moved around the country to other jails.
"Shipped out" it's called. If it's anyone of note it's an armed one.
Same as bed watches where a prisoner has to go to hospital.
Imagine sitting in a hospital room with armed police around you.
I did a few of them in my time.

I have mentioned Control and restraint in this book a few times.
Sometimes that goes out of the window dependant on the situation.
I recall one evening on Red spur.
I was chatting to a prisoner on the twos landing.
A prisoner came running at me, I still to this day don't know why.
He was almost on me before I noticed.
I quickly turned, put my leg up, Thud.
I caught him between the legs. He went down like a sack of potatoes.
The prisoner next to me said
" Wow, what a shot Mr D" even he was impressed.
Sometimes you've got to defend yourself.
I didn't know if the attacking prisoner was armed and I didn't have the time to use C and R methods.
Self defence.

Prior to me leaving C wing onto my next venture at Whitemoor I was patrolling Green spur. A lot of prisoners were at the workshops.
Unbeknown to me, 2 prisoners had booked out kitchen knives.

These knives were not sharp and were basically vegetable knives.

All was quiet. You could literally hear a pin drop.

Cleaners were busy mopping etc.. I was the only officer on green spur as there were limited prisoners unlocked.

There was one member of staff on red spur. My colleague on red spur at this time was almost retirement age.

He was walking about the spur and on the twos landing.

All of a sudden you could hear a massive clatter coming from red spur twos landing kitchen.

The two prisoners that had booked out the knives must've had a disagreement whilst cooking and decided to go for it.

My colleague hit the alarm bell.

They both slashed at each other, one had a pan as well and was hitting the other with it.

Then they turned, both of them,on my colleague. Jumping on him, punching and kicking him.

There was quite a lot of blood by the time I'd ran from Green spur to red spur. I restrained one of them whilst other staff restrained the other.

My colleague got up and dusted himself down.

1997 and my time on C wing was over.

2 years on the wing.

Eventful and in a way it was sad to leave but it's also refreshing to have a change in environment and routine.

But before I carry on I'll leave you with an eerie story.

Whilst on C wing I was teaching some prisoners to become wing barbers.

Due to Whitemoors status as a maximum security Prison it was difficult to get Hairdressers to the Prison.

I didn't have the time due to staff shortages and family life.

Although , as aforementioned I cut staffs hair.
One regular to get his haircut was a Prisoner called "Tate."
He was my landing cleaner on green spur.
He must've had haircuts every 2 weeks.

I was in March town centre speaking to Miranda from my wing
when a black Limo parked right next to us. Out came Tate,
Tucker and Rolfe.
They'd hired a limo for Tates release.

Tate came over to Miranda and I. He gave us a hug and asked
if we wanted to go to the pub.
We declined.
He then said
" What will i do Tony? I'll have to pay for my haircuts now"
In the next breath he said
" Mind you, I won't have a head by Christmas"

Them words will forever haunt me.
On December 6th that year Tate, Tucker and Rolfe were
murdered, Tate shot in the head in Rettendon in Essex.
The Essex Boys.
Later on to be immortalised in a film starring Sean Bean as
Tate.

A massive thank you to all C Wing staff who taught me the
ropes of the job.
A fantastic mob . Great staff, and I hope you are all doing ok.
Also to " Bullet" who saved my arse during the riot.

Exceptional, to The end.

I returned to Newbold Revel again. This time to do a course to work in the SSU. The Special Secure Unit.

As aforementioned this Houses Exceptional Risk Category A prisoners.
The highest risk in the English prison system.

Not accommodated in a 4 star Daventry hotel this time as the accommodation at Newbold had been refurbished.
The course itself focussed on counter conditioning and was mainly classroom work but there were trips up the road to The Union Jack pub as well as Newbolds own bar .
Nothing as rowdy as 2 years prior.

Talking of Rowdy. That was the nickname of our new SSU senior officer who was on this course.
Rowdy was a soft spoken guy from the North of Scotland. He nicknamed me "Scorrie" which is a Northern Scottish name for seagull.
Not sure if that was a compliment.

Rowdy was an ex Falklands veteran who was an ex Marine.
We had some laughs during the course.
One such laugh was our orienteering day out on the Malvern hills.
There were 4 of us from Whitemoor on the course.
One being ex Royal engineers.

Now this guy ,on me observing him in the past ,Patrolled a landing like he was patrolling the streets of Belfast in the 1970s.
That walking then turning to look behind him kind of movement. All that was missing was an SLR rifle.

The course included orienteering with maps.
The ex sapper was straight in there.
"Easy this, I'm an expert on maps"

Now I wasn't unfit but getting up the first mound of the
Malvern's nearly did me in.
Rowdy was up the mound like a ferret.
When I reached the top ,Rowdy put his hand into his rucksack
and produced a bottle of whisky and 2 glasses.
A real welcoming sight.
By the time we got half way we were half cut. Sharing stories
as we walked admiring the scenery atop the Malverns.
Just after halfway we bumped into another pair from the
course.
One was a Jamaican lad from HMP Belmarsh.
He had 100% proof rum with him and offered us a drink of that
as well.
If nothing else Rowdy and I were warm.

We finally ,after 3 hours got to the bus at the end that was
picking us up.
We all mustered.
All bar the Sapper and his walking partner.
He was called via radio from the walk coordinator.
" Come in Charlie 5"
No answer first time.
" Charlie 5 do you copy?"
There was a brief silence.
"Erm, erm , yes I copy, we're lost and stuck in a mudbog"
Well, we fell about laughing.
The map expert ,ex Engineer was lost.! The guy who knew
cartography like the back of his hand was up to his knees in
mud.

The route he'd taken was nowhere near what was on our maps. He took some stick.

The SSU had been completely revamped since the infamous IRA escape . There were always rumours about how that happened.
Some say the gun used in the escape was put there by Irish builders, some say staff brought the gun in.
During the escape a dog handler got a bullet to his shoulder as the 6 men tried to get away.
They say staff were conditioned to the hilt, poor searching , no go areas created by prisoners etc..
We will never know the full story but anyway, it happened.

Getting into the SSU as a member of staff was hard enough so chances of getting out of it were nil by this time.
I won't go into detail for obvious security reasons but I reckon Fort Knox would be easier.
If you weren't on duty in there, you weren't getting in without permission from within its walls.
It was a prison within a prison.

The SSU wasn't as relaxed as the wings, it wasn't austere but near enough.
Everyone's movement was carefully observed, staff included.
We wore personal alarms which registered where we were inside the unit at all times. Plus we walked around in pairs.

As soon as I started duty there I had ex C and D wing prisoners saying to me
" We shouldn't be in here boss"
" We didn't plot any escape Mr D"
" We didn't know each other until now"
Hold your thought on that last quote.

If I had a quid for every time I heard this I'd be living in a mansion overlooking the beach in the Bahamas.

When I say everything was monitored, I mean everything,including Prisoners phone calls.
We had one prisoner who kept saying Rover is missing you to his girlfriend.
We were thinking Rover was a dog until the prisoner said
" Rovers bursting in my pants"
We burst at this. Obviously " Rover" was his penis.
On returning into the unit from listening my colleague Paul and I started talking about dogs.
I said " I miss my old dog"
Paul said " What was his name?"
" Rover " I replied..
The prisoner just looked at us.
" Rover was a big big hairy dog, I miss stroking him" I said.
The prisoner blushed and walked away.
He knew.

I worked in the censors a lot there where I had to read prisoners correspondence.
That was fun.
Reading all the sloppy letters, some sprayed with cheap perfume that choked the back of your throat. Part of censoring was checking for drugs in letters. It's amazing what you can find under a stamp.
I remember my dad telling me he found a £10 note under a postage stamp when he worked at HMP Perth.
You always opened mail wearing gloves in case the letters were laced. There has been cases of officers hospitalised due to handling mail laced with LSD which had seeped into their skin.

So, I was on nights.

Nightshift is 7 nights on 7 off.

Nights does get boring as the whole unit is locked down.

There are 2 staff in the unit.

An SSU Officer and a member of DST (Dedicated Search Team).

I decided to read some prisoners reports.

I was always quite alert when looking into stuff at work.

I was reading files on the C and D wing prisoners who had recently been placed in the unit.

I'd hit the jackpot.

Remember earlier I said hold your thought on that last quote, " We didn't know each other until now"

Well I read differently whilst reading these files.

There had been a course run for Prisoners.

Every Prisoner that had been on the course from C and D wings were the ones in the SSU protesting their innocence in an escape plot, and guess who was supervising the course?

Yes,my old colleague who was serving time in Prison for trafficking drugs into Whitemoor.

I put 2 and 2 together.

The plot was hatched on that course.

I passed all the info onto Security.

The security Governor was over the moon with this.

It confirmed everything.

Sometimes being nosey is a good thing.

All them times they said they didn't know each other prior to the SSU was bullshit.

My work as an officer in general hadn't gone unnoticed.

One of the Senior Officers in the SSU and a Governor took me into an office.

They asked me to go and take the Senior Officers exam and go for promotion.

I decided against it.

Not that I lacked ambition,but not for me.

Yes, it's more money and career advancement but to me my bread and butter was on the landings.

I didn't want an office job.

I never went for promotion in that job.

A funny moment in the SSU was when the PO came into the unit.

The one I argued with about safety in numbers after the hot fat incident on C wing.

Ian and myself heard the Senior officer ask the PO if he wanted a coffee.

He obliged.

Ian and I started flicking sweeteners into the kettle. I reckon we put over 30 sweeteners in.

Watching the PO take a sip and then proceeding to spit the coffee out over the briefing room wall was side splitting for us pair.

Later on we were pulled by the SO saying

" I know it was one of you two or both that did this"

Even he laughed though.

Just desserts PO .

Rowdy, the other Senior Officer had some sense of humour.

We got a prisoner in called Kulunk.

One evening prisoners were banging up for the night.

Rowdy turned to the prisoner and said

" Go on, make a noise like your name"

I got it straight away. It's called an onomatepia .

If you still haven't got it refer back to the prisoners name .

We had one Prisoner in there who got a 40 year sentence for drug importation.

That's a big stretch.

That's more than an average murderer gets.

It's the biggest sentence I'd ever seen bar Lifers.

For a guy doing that amount of time he was pleasant enough to work with.

Most Prisoners in the SSU were pleasant enough at that time.

We had 2 co defendants in there together.

They got a video sent in with various things on the video.

Included was One of the Kray twins funerals, one of their daughters weddings , another couple of London heavies funerals plus a few family things. 18ths, 21sts etc..

My colleague Richie having already seen the contents waited till the 2 prisoners were in the room eagerly awaiting to watch said video and announced

" For your entertainment today we have 4 funerals and a wedding"

On hearing this I nearly wet myself with laughter.

You could clearly see the Prisoners were not amused.

We had an American and a Colombian in there. They were like best buddies. Very close.

They were akin to the Lone Ranger and Tonto. Always side by side.

I don't know what happened but one day all I heard was

" I kill you, I kill you"

2 of us went running to find the Columbia with his hands round the Americans throat.

The Colombian guy was still screaming at him in his Colombian accent.

We restrained him and took him to his cell.

I asked the Colombian what had happened?
His English wasn't great.

" He cook a da chicken wrong" still visibly raging.

I burst out laughing.
What is it with Chicken?
It started a riot on C wing, now it's causing fights in the SSU.
I spoke to the kitchen PO one day and said
" Please take chicken off the menu, it's causing hell in here"

During the time on the SSU my marriage started to crumble.
A lot of Officers marriages suffered.
At that time the statistics were
Police 1 in 3 Marriages suffered.
Prison Service 1 in 2.
Not good is it?

I briefly moved out and into lodgings.
My landlord was an SO at Whitemoor, Dave. Dave was and
still is an outstanding human being.
Also in the lodgings was my SSU colleague Paul.
Heartbreak Hotel we called it.
I think that Officers married to Officers is probably the best
way.
They understand the shifts, the stress we suffer, and the
environment we work in.
I still thought back to the riot and how close I was to meeting
my maker whoever that may have been , which wasn't helping
my state of mind at the time.

During my time there we had guitar jamming sessions.
Dave had recorded in the 60s and had played on the same bill
as The Beatles.

He had Polaroid pictures of the Fab 4.
I told him they were worth a fortune, he wouldn't have parted with them.
I suppose memories are worth a lot more than money.
We'd spend hours playing guitar, Paul doing the vocals.
Great times. But bad times if you know what I mean. I had small children, as did Paul.
I couldn't stop thinking about my kids.
I moved back to the marital home.

My time came to an end in the SSU in 1998.
You can only spend 15 months in the unit at any one time.
It was pretty uneventful , probably due to its tight security.
Nothing much went on.

A Wing.

I got moved to A Wing.

A wing was a Vulnerable Prisoner wing.
Sex offenders, debtors from the main wings ,and what were known as Prison Grasses.
Grasses we're perceived as being as bad as sex offenders as far as Prisoners are concerned.
I was put on the same spur as the notorious Serial Killer Dennis Nielsen.

This guy was certainly weird.
He had a piano keyboard.
All he played was music that resembled the organ music from the horror films known as " Dr Phibes"
Constant drowning organ sounds.

He was , as portrayed recently in the series "Des". Superbly played by David Tennant I might add.
His cell always stank probably the same as his whole flat with all its cadavers in it.

He wasn't a clean person.
He was dry as sticks, no humour about him and I don't think I ever saw him smile.
He had this blank look about him, eyes as dark as a great white shark.
No emotion.

He very rarely spoke and when he did it was just verbal shite.
We'd ask him stuff like
" what does human flesh taste like?"
"Are you the pink panther?"
As Donald Neilson was known as the black Panther.
His answer to the flesh tasting was
" I may have killed people and caressed them, I never ate them"
Mmmm , I wonder.
His killings were akin to Jeffrey Dahmers.

Nielsen killed for company as his book suggests. Sat corpses in armchairs next to him, cuddled them, had them in his bed.
I'd have hated to have been the drainage company going out to unblock his old flats drainage system.
Torsos and heads floating etc.…
He had the smug attitude , sort of look at me, I'm world famous.
To me , he was just another Prison number with no status whatsoever.

The wing was totally different to C wing.

I found it dirtier, not unclean but maybe it was the clientele on that wing that made it feel that way.

We had one prisoner that used to sit on the taps in his sink and move up and down for a sexual thrill.

He got the nickname "Taps"

He really was a vile individual who's crime I won't repeat, but it was sickening to the core. He's dead now.

Good riddance.

We had Duffy, the railway rapist who was another deplorable individual.

There were so many that I'd be writing this book for another couple of years.

One day we heard a scream from one of the spurs. A prisoner was punching a female member of staff. This in my book was a no no.

You do not hit a female.

I lost it and on decking the prisoner I made sure he wasn't going to enjoy it.

I wouldn't call it red mist but I was raging.

Red mist is when anger determines your actions basically and you go overboard.

I used correct c and r methods but made sure the prisoner felt it.

I detest any form of violence toward a female.

Whilst on A wing I had applied for a transfer to HMP Frankland.

Another Cat A Maximum security prison on the outskirts of Durham city.

I applied to move to get my marriage back on track.

Fresh start.

I got my transfer.

It was goodbye to 4 years at Whitemoor.
On my final day staff jumped me, put me in locks, threw me in a cold bath which prisoners had ran ,wrote obscenities and I mean Obscenities all over my white shirt then hosed me with the fire hose.
I still had to go to one of our female Governors offices before I left the Prison.
I walked into her office.
She burst out laughing.
I was soaked to the bone.
She was reading all the writing on my shirt and giggling.
" There's one thing Tony, you will certainly be missed here"

I'm sure the detail office would miss me most.
I left with over 100 hours due to Time off in Lieu. (Toil) as we called it.
This being due to staff shortages that I'd covered.

I'd certainly miss Whitemoor.

A big thank you to everyone I worked with there.
There are far too many to mention.
For the laughter, the tears and the memories,good and bad.

Chapter 3

" The Geordie Mafia?"

I've called this chapter "The Geordie Mafia" due to comments from the documentary " Inside Monster Mansion" which was shown on Channel 5 and inspired me to write this book.
One of Frankland ex prisoners called the staff this name.

HMP Frankland is situated on the outskirts of Durham city next to a housing estate which was once Europe's largest estate. Newton Hall.

It, like Whitemoor holds Category A and B Prisoners.

It sits next door to HMP Low Newton. Now a female Prison.

I started on G Wing in September 1999 at what they call the top end.

A, B, C and D wings were at the bottom end.

F and G wings at the top.

I hadn't even been on the wing for 5 minutes when an ex Whitemoor Prisoner came right up to me. Shook my hand and asked how I was.

He then said

" How's that Officer getting on that got jailed for trafficking drugs"

My ex colleague.

I said as far as I knew he was still in jail.

He then said

" Where do you think that prisoner got your personal details from?"

I asked him how he knew this

" I was in the cell when he gave them to the prisoner"

I was raging.

I asked why he never told me at the time.

" I was the only witness to it. If it had come out I'd have been a grass"

I understood.

That just shows how colleagues can put your life and your families life in danger.

I hated bent staff.

Always did.

G wing had 2 landings and was like an L shape. The main centre office was on the ones.
On entering G wing you were immediately on the ones landing
.

Some of the prisoners there I knew quite well from before so it wasn't like I was a stranger. Some of them wanted to be there, some of them were ghosted there.
Ghosted is where they are told to pack immediately to be moved to another prison. They don't know where they are going. Usually for security reasons.

I got to know the staff pretty quickly as the north east folk are very friendly. A great bunch of guys and lasses that made me feel welcome.
I got my new nickname on Day 1.
I saw a prisoner running up the landing.
I shouted out
" Walk, don't run or I'll place you on report"
My colleague Colin said
" Ho man, you're Dangerous" in his Geordie accent.
Then he laughed and said
" That's your nickname now, Dangerous"
So it stuck.

The prisoners on the wing , as they did at Whitemoor sat with each other according to areas they came from.
Newcastle, Sunderland, Bradford/Leeds, Scottish , Irish etc….
The Geordies seemed to have the bigger majority , second only to the Mackems who are from Sunderland, then the Smoggies who are Middlesbrough.
It seemed to be the way of things in Prison.
Sit with your own crew.

There were quite a few Manchester contingent on G wing as well , including Paul Massey who basically ran Salford.
I knew Massey from Whitemoor.

The Irish ones we got in were the IRA mob ,who if they'd succeeded would have blown out Londons power supply for months.
Their plot was foiled luckily.
One of them was only 21. Very ,very quiet individuals.
Sometimes the quiet ones are the evil ones.
My previous dealings with such Prisoners were that they kept themselves to themselves and didn't really mix.
They rarely spoke to staff either unless they needed something.

I once nicked an IRA prisoner who refused to go on the nicking unless he could wear full Paramilitary regalia due to him thinking himself, as they all did , as Prisoners of War.

G wing was a fairly relaxed place to work but by god if a fight broke out it proper went.
I remember a Geordie lad and a scouser going for it outside the wing one day.
You'd have paid for ringside seats to watch that one.
There was claret everywhere, they'd broken each other's noses.
We waited till they'd kind of stopped it themselves.
As so often ,if you intervene too quickly and I've seen it ,where both turn on you instead.

Pool cues were great weapons as were pool balls.
A prisoner on G wing got a sock of pool balls cracked over his head one day. It knocks you clean out. Sparko.

I think the worst assault on G wing was when a Geordie lad assaulted the young IRA prisoner.

The young lad was sat in the TV room.

The Geordie lad went into the room.

Myself and my colleague Glenn were sat at a table next to the TV toom taking Prisoners applications.

There was an almighty crash.

All I heard shouted was " Im an ex Para"

We ran in and dragged the Geordie lad off the young IRA guy ,who's face had basically been split open.

The Geordie lad was screaming

" I'm an ex Para ,he deserves to die"

Obviously references to the Belfast troubles.

We restrained the Geordie lad and took him to segregation.

I never found out if he was an ex Para or not.

Guaranteed he'd be a marked man by the IRA though.

The lads n lasses I worked with were top notch.

Professional and most had the same " Firm but Fair" attitude as myself.

There were some characters I worked with . One such character was Frankie McLaughlin.

Frankie had been in the job a long time. He started at Medomsley near Consett way way back ,then HMP Durham, then Frankland.

Real old school screw he was.

I will never forget his antics.

Even prisoners couldn't help loving him.

One time I was on duty with him.

A prisoner was sending a poster out to family and had asked the art department for a poster tube.

The said poster tube arrived on the wing via internal mail.

Frankie brought the poster tube onto the wing.

" Mac" he shouted to the prisoner.

" Yes Frankie" he replied.

Frankie said " This your tube?"

Mac replied

" Yes, I ordered it from the Art department"

Frankie hit the poster tube off the railings on the wing. It broke in half.

" You've got 2 tubes now" Frankie laughed.

Mac was incensed but then took the two bits of tube and laughed.

As he walked away he said,

" only you Frankie, only you".

Frankie was the king of the centre office tannoy.

We had a prisoner on there who resembled a rat facially, so he was nicknamed "Ratboy" by prisoners.

Every lunch time after lock up if Frankie was in the centre office he'd put the tannoy on every so often and say

" Squeak , Squeak, Raaatboy"

The whole wing would laugh.

Including Ratboy.

I remember a Governor coming on the wing. I was sat with Frankie on the 2s landing.

The Governor said

" How are you Frankie?"

Frankie replied,

" I was fuckin fine till you came on the wing thanks Governor"

He had a way with words.

He once sat with a piece of paper doing maths.

I asked him what he was doing.

" I've just sat and worked out that at roll correct ,walking to the gate from this wing every year it costs us over 15 lost hours"

I burst out laughing.

"Roll correct" is when prisoners are locked away and staff can leave duty for lunch or end of shift.

F and G wings was a bit of a hike to the gate so Frankies calculations were probably right.

I've mentioned Prison humour.

It is dark, sick and twisted but it kept us sane in a way.

I lost my Uncle whilst working on G Wing.

The staff were told of this. It happened on the Saturday night.

This was the Monday afternoon and I was back at work.

Take this how you will but on hearing it Frankie said,

" You alright Dangerous?"

I told him I was in a bit of shock as my uncle basically died in my arms whilst visiting me.

He then patted me on the back and said ,

" I hope you got his watch and his wallet mate"

Now, to some of you who read this you'll think , sick bastard.

But no, I actually laughed for the first time since it happened.

Prison humour. It's how we dealt with things. Frankie was a master of that.

Frankie, you'll be up there somewhere giving somebody pelters.

Rest in peace mate.

Two other particularly funny things of note came from a female Senior officer who was guesting on G Wing within minutes.

The first one was she took some black boot polish and blackened the earpiece of the phone hoping someone answered it.

A couple of minutes later it rang.

Who picked it up?

Yes you've got it, the female Senior Officer herself.

Then what followed you couldn't make up.

The chaplaincy had rung up asking if a Prisoner could be informed that his brother had been murdered the night before.

To which the female S O replied

" He's been murdered?, what? Dead?"

I don't know anyone who has been murdered and survived.

Not only was she red faced but also black eared.

G wing was a fairly quiet place in all fairness but one particular incident I remember was on G1 .

A prisoner I knew from Whitemoor was on the wing.

This guy was quite a big individual.

He was also very unstable.

He had been playing pool with other prisoners when he just flipped.

He took a pool cue and cracked it over my colleague Colin's head with some force.

We immediately restrained him on the floor and got him cuffed.

Whilst on the floor he shouted to me

" Duncan, you're next"

He never got me.

Colin was on an escort a couple of years later to a secure mental health unit.

A guy sat next to him and said

" Do you remember me?"

Colin didn't recognise him at all. He'd changed so much.
Smart dressed, lost weight etc…
" I'm the guy that hit you with a pool cue and I'd like to
apologise for what I did"
The Prisoner shook hands with Colin.

In the Service we don't get any mental health training
whatsoever ,so when a Prisoner comes in with varying issues
we didn't know how to deal with them.
Frankland had loads.
One who ate his own faeces off the floor.
Later on Frankland had a DSPD unit built.
"Dangerous and severe personality Disorder unit" .
Obviously realising the need for this.
The staff working on there got the training they so desperately
needed.
A welcome sight for Frankland.

Nights on G wing were good.
Going round with a mobile phone detector. A device that could
read mobile signals at close range, pinpointing which cell was
using.

I remember one night I got a great signal outside a cell.
I contacted the Orderly Officer, a Principal Officer who was in
charge of the prison.
He brought 2 staff up with him. We went to the cell.
Oscar 1, the orderly Officer put his key in the door and the 3 of
us were in the cell.
The prisoner was startled.
I told him we were giving him a cell search.
Searching is a delicate matter.
In Maximum security jails the prisoner, on suspicion of
concealing anything performs a strip search.

Top half first then bottom half.
At no point is an individual in a naked state.
We could also ask them to squat if reasonable suspicion.

I asked the prisoner
" Do you have anything concealed about your person before I
conduct this strip search?
" No Boss was the reply"
Just as he said it, a vibrating sound could be heard from his
nether regions.
Immediately I said
" Well you're either using a dildo or that's a mobile phone,
hand it over or we will use force to obtain it"
He started to move his hands toward his trousers to push the
mobile phone up his rectum, but by this time we'd restrained
him . During this ,the phone had dropped out of the bottom of
his trousers.

Another night I noticed a large amount of sugar outside a cell
scattered on the floor.
I did my first check. There was obviously a crunching sound
beneath my boots.
I thought mmmmm I think I'll quietly sweep that up later.
Obviously the prisoner was up to something and if he heard a
crunch he'd know I was in his vicinity.
I waited till the landings were fairly quiet , got a brush and
quietly swept the sugar away.
About 20 minutes later, just in time I looked into his cell.
There he was jacking a substance into his arm.
I crept away , contacted Oscar 1 the orderly Officer and we
searched him and his cell.
I found a small bag with brown in it.
Later confirmed as Heroin.

Turns out a Prisoner had stole a couple of syringes from Healthcare.

Heroin isn't just available on the streets.

I've found copious amounts of drugs but that's another story for later in this book.

I think my worst on G wing was a prisoner who at 6.30 am got on his cell call button.

It was coming to the end of my shift.

I went to the cell.

" What's up?" I asked.

The prisoner looked at me.

" I need a nurse"

I said " It's 6.30 in the morning, can you wait till 7.30 when the day staff are on?"

He moved away from the flap window.

I'm not joking, there was blood everywhere, you could see some of it was congealed.

Immediately I radioed for medical assistance.

They were quick to the scene. Along with a dog handler as Cat A prisoners cannot be unlocked without dog handler presence. We got in the cell. There were clumps of congealed blood, they resembled small jellyfish. He was grey in colour.

He was rushed away in an ambulance under escort.

I checked the Cat A's religiously every hour. I saw him moving in his bed throughout the night so had no concerns,but found out later he'd been cutting at the veins in his legs under the sheets since early morning.

He was damn lucky he survived.

There were a lot of self harm incidents in prison. I opened a cell door on G wing to find a prisoner had sliced his entire torso with razor blades.

If these guys don't tell you they need help , how are you to know?

My worst one was on the hospital wing.
I said I'd do a week of nights.
Bonus is you get 7 days off after it.
Now this prisoner was a complete menace.
He did stuff for his own amusement to try to wind staff up.

On night one and two that week he was very quiet. Night 3 was horrendous.
He kept pressing his cell call button. He must've hit it about 8 times by this point. Each time we have to attend it.
It is supposed to be pressed in emergencies.
This prisoner didn't have an emergency at all.
He was doing it to wind me up.
Over 100 times he pressed it.

The next thing, he asked for the Samaritans phone.
I got it brought to the hospital wing.
He was handed the phone.
The only number that the phone has access to is The Samaritans themselves, like a direct line.
If a prisoner asks it's our obligation to give them this phone.

The prisoner got the phone, then blocked the viewing panel so we couldn't see in.
His cell inside had a camera as he was being watched.
He then put wet tissue on the camera lens inside the cell.
There was only myself and a nurse on the wing at the time.
I gave him a direct order to remove the tissue from the camera and his viewing panel.
I got a resounding " Fuck off Duncan"

I don't know what he did to that phone but the next thing I got a call on the wing.
The prisoner had somehow tampered with the phone and managed to ring the main gate of the prison.

I went outside his cell and told him again to remove all the tissue.
" Give me a couple of minutes" he said.
I waited. I could hear noises inside his cell.
He removed the tissue blocking observation flap.

Now I've seen a lot of things in my life but not this.
He had ripped his cheek open with blades and actually stuck his tongue through the hole in his cheek.
He got rushed to hospital.
Turns out he had earlier slit a pouch into his cheek to hide 2 razor blades in.
This method is often used in jails to hide things.
But I had never seen anyone till then open up their cheek and poke their tongue through it.
So there, a tongue in cheek perspective on a Prisoner.

I was on G wing for around two and a half years , then went on to the Security department at Frankland.
This was working with intelligence and generally going around the jail for staff info etc..
Working with Security Information reports , checking wing log books and looking for anything of note.
I enjoyed working on Security.
It got me around the jail a lot.
We also covered the visits hall.

I recall being on visits one day with a female colleague.
A female visitor came up to me and said

" What are you doing this weekend?"
I replied,
" Probably working, Why?"
She then said she liked the look of me and wondered if I
wanted to go out.
I burst out laughing, so did my female colleague.
I said thanks ,but no thanks and promptly put a Security
Information report in.
No Tinder in them days .

Whilst on G wing one day doing security checks I got
information that a Prisoner was going to get sprung from an
escort.
Luckily , the info was right and it didn't happen. The Escort
was moved to another date.
The safety to staff on an escort is at risk anytime they go out.
You don't know who walks among the general public.

3 Staff at Frankland were escorting a Prisoner once to
Newcastle General Hospital.
As they exited the van with a Cat A Prisoner they were faced
with 3 gunmen, demanding they release him or get shot.
They released him ,as any officer would faced with that. Your
only armour being a white shirt.
Yep, I'd have done the same.
Them guys are traumatised to this day as one of the gunmen
was about to pull the trigger.

You see, no one sees what goes on in a prison.
It's like a secret society within 4 walls that you don't get to
look into.
TV documentaries give a very small insight into the day to day
running of a jail.
It's not like that.

It's a complex environment ,that unless you work there you just wouldn't understand.

No one sees how staff suffer.

A lot say nothing, even at home you don't say anything as your partner, if not in the job, just doesn't understand.

Hence why I said earlier marriages suffer.

People deal with stress in different ways.

I, like many started to drink heavier than I should have. Mainly to sleep better.

You can't just switch off when you get home. There's all the Adrenalin from that day still pumping inside you.

It lasts for hours, keeps you awake etc....

PTSD wasn't a word used in the Prison service till recently really.

In 2002 my marriage broke.

The day I watched my kids get driven back to Scotland was absolutely heartbreaking.

I broke down several times a day for a long time after that.

I wonder how life would've turned out had I not joined the prison service?

I often asked myself this.

I've been through riots, attempted assaults etc.....Saying goodbye to my kids is the worst thing I've ever went through.

I had to crack on.

The drinking subsided and I got on with my job.

I had a run in with a prisoner once that the end result incensed me.

He came out of the Chapel in the jail.

My job was to run down search all prisoners leaving the chapel.

The Prisoner attempted to assault me, he failed, but did try.
He sped off.
I called on the radio as to what had happened.
Staff then caught up with him and escorted him to the wing.
You can't help who you know.
One prisoner I knew from the Perth area, who was a customer
of mine when I was a hairdresser was on the same wing as this
Irish prisoner.
The prisoner asked the Prisoner what he knew about me. In
particular what football team I supported.
I am admittedly a Glasgow Rangers fan.
The prisoner jumped on this.

The adjudication took place.
Sadly, the only witnesses to this were one Officer, who said he
never saw it.
He did see it and loads of prisoners witnessed it.
They weren't going to grass on him. I was out on a limb really.
The Governor got me to read my evidence for attempted
assault.
He then questioned the prisoner who pled not guilty.
The prisoner then said
 "Mr Duncan nicked me because he supports Rangers and I'm
a Celtic fan"

Immediately I said that was a lie.
In my eyes this had nothing to do with Football or religion.
I have many Celtic supporting friends.

This was to do with an attempted assault on myself.
The Governor gave the prisoner a not guilty verdict.
This Governor was soft as shit anyway. Prisoners friend we
used to call him.
I was raging.

I actually said and I quote
" You've just made me the biggest fucking bigot in the jail I'm taking this further"
I went to the number one Governor who went through the other Governor who had to apologise to me.
I can assure you now. I would place any prisoner on report for attempted assault on myself , staff or another prisoner regardless of Creed, colour, religion no matter what.
That's that put straight for the book as they say.

Dedicated Search Team (DST)

I continued on Security until I joined the DST.
DST teams were set up in Category A Prisons in the aftermath of the Whitemoor escape.
Highly trained to search cells, inside and outside of prisons, vehicles etc sometimes using Specialist equipment.

Off I went to Newbold Revel yet again.
2 weeks of specialist searching.
Bit of drinking of an evening but I didn't go overboard with it.
We got to use some of the new hi tec equipment that was available for all DST units.
Some of it was outstanding, built to search underwater etc.. a bit like an ROV used by marine biologists.
Some great pieces of kit.

On my return I was going to work with some of the funniest, most mischievious staff I'd ever worked with.
It consisted of the biggest cranks at Frankland, and I mean that in a humorous way.
You couldn't have put a funnier mob together like that again.
From day one it was a laugh.

In the mornings we'd be greeted with " Supertramp, Breakfast in America" on our CD player. Everyday that album was played at least twice.
First thing we would supervise workshop movement.
Searching prisoners going to the workshops.
Usually there'd be nothing of note going into the workshops so generally it was quiet.
After workshops we went out to wings to search cells.

We had sheets with designated cells. We had to search every cell within a month.
That's A, B, C, D, F and G wings.
That's a lot of searches a month ,not forgetting areas such as Workshops and other departments.

We made searching as much of a laugh as we could.
Some cells stank.
Unclean prisoners was common.
I used to tell them
" You're cell is stinking, get it cleaned and get some soap"
I never held back in that job.
I remember saying to one prisoner
" I'm gonna put a pig in your cell as an air freshener" it was honking.

I was reminded recently that during cell searches with him ,I couldn't resist picking up guitars in cells.
I taught my colleague Steve to Play " Peaches" by the Stranglers.
I played on every guitar in the jail in my time on DST I reckon.
There were some DST that would have a shot on the Prisoners PlayStations.
Yes they had them.

We had some great finds.
An imitation gun made of wood inside a mattress , drugs, weapons.
I remember being on A wing. I don't know why but we were sat in their TV room. I put my hand down the inside of a chair. I pulled out a prison made tattoo gun straight away. We then checked all the chairs. Weapons, drug paraphernalia , burnt foil ,all sorts. That was just in the TV room. Some haul we had.
On searching 2 cells that time I found drugs inside a pillowcase and the next cell I saw the toilet was slightly dislodged and found a litre of hooch stashed behind the toilet.

Hooch is prison made alcohol. It contains fruit and yeast normally.
It ferments.
The smell of it alone is enough to put you off along with the sight of rotting fruit bobbing around at the top of the container. The containers were the ones used to hold cleaning fluids. They'd wash them out and begin the process.
If I ever searched a cell that I thought contained more fruit than normal in it, I removed the fruit.
Absolutely foul stuff hooch was.

One serious find , bar weapons and drugs were photographs of a currently serving female officer at the jail in a Prisoners cell. She was in varying states of undress.
Yet another colleague getting involved with a prisoner.
What are they thinking?
She was sacked.
Not long after it I was in the Metro Centre near Newcastle .
There she was hand in hand with the ex Prisoner.

DST Locker Wars.

Not all wars in jail are with prisoners.
Our own battle began on DST with each other.
I don't mean war in a bad way.

It all started with one locker.
The locker belonged to Johnny on DST.
Johnny went on holiday abroad.
During his vacation another DST colleague went along to the
brick workshop, acquired some bricks and cement, and
proceeded to build a brick wall inside Johnnys locker. There
was a picture of this with the Number one Governor smiling
and pointing at the brickwork.
So on his return flight a stewardess who knew one of the DST
went up to Johnny on the plane and asked if he was a
bricklayer
" No" was Johnnys reply.
She basically said oh and left it at that.

On Johnnys return to work you can only imagine his face on
opening his locker to see a brick wall built into it.
Priceless.
That was the start.
The next day my colleague who had bricked up the locker
opened his.
Johnny had rigged the water hose to the tap, got behind Daves
locker and put the end of the hose inside the locker.
When Dave opened his locker he was met with a jet of water to
the face.
Now the wars started heating up.
One of my DST colleagues went into the gym.
On a lunchtime we could use the Prison gym.

My colleague finished his session and went and got changed back into his uniform. He pulled in his black combat trousers only to find half the leg of his trousers had been cut off.
We didn't know what we were walking into entering the DST bunker.
I've been blasted with fire hoses, foam from extinguishers etc but the worst of all was losing my tobacco.

We were on G wing searching.
I finished my search and put my jacket on.
It weighed a ton.
I put my hands in my jacket pockets. They were full of gunge.
It was Prison marmalade.
My colleague Collin had done it, and shredded all my tobacco , filters etc into my pocketfuls of the gungy marmalade.
I was raging at first but hey it was a DST war.
Next day I brought in a tin of tuna. I walked past Collin and emptied the full contents on his lap. Stinking tuna and he had to walk around all day with it.
He wasn't amused but knew it was in retaliation for the tobacco incident.

The locker wars heightened.
Cut up clothes, soakings with buckets of water and hoses,DST staff jumping out on you from cupboards etc..
I went on a weeks leave , came back to find 4 open tins of tuna inside my locker that had been there for a week.
Thanks Collin.
The ultimate, and the reason it stopped was some DST took another DST colleagues car a few miles from the jail.
Parked it up and put bags of dog shit inside the car.
Bearing in mind it was summertime.

To the snowflakes nowadays it would all be classed as bullying.

To us it was humour up until the car incident.

Staff humour is very dark in jails as I mentioned earlier.

It has to be. What others find horrifying , we found funny.

From day to day we didn't know what we were facing, if we were getting home on time or if we'd get home safe and without injury.

It's not your average 9-5 job.

Prison is 24/7.

I got a call out on DST at 2am one morning.

Turns out someone had thrown a firearm over the wall.

Luckily it didn't get near the actual jail. It landed in the perimeter.

Yes, it was only a starter pistol used for sporting events like races but imagine being faced with it in the wrong hands.

Would you know the difference?

We used to do searches during the night as well if needed.

I was recently reminded by a former colleague of a night search.

Looking back it was funny.

Here's what Johnny said about that search.

" There was one time on G Wing when we went covertly to open a couple of doors looking for mobile phones.

It was the lad that had tortured the officer at HMP Castington.

There was Me, you and another Officer.

We went to open the door quietly.

Your keys hit the door like the ghost of Christmas past.

It alerted the prisoner into barricading to stop us from getting in.

It was described as the attack of the tomato heads.
The prisoner got that much of a shock when we broke through the barricade that he froze and put his hands up in the air.
Me and you were like Rick and Vyvyan from the Young ones when he was confronted with his drug taking ways.
Johnny and I never held back at times like that.

Johnny also reminded me of a trip we did to search HMP Wakefield.
I did a lot of talking to the porcelain telephone that night.
I was absolutely pissed out of my head and had to search at Wakefield the next morning.
That saying, " Never on a school night"is so true.
I hadn't had a hangover like that for a lot of years.

I was team leader one day. We took turns at this on DST.
 Trust mine to be the day they ordered a full lockdown of the prison.
I was basically in charge of coordinating the whole search from putting teams together to dealing with finds
It's quite a bit of work.
Basically planning who would search where, what areas needed searched , what staff and resources I had to do this.
And it had to be completed by midday.

It was 7.30 am when I got told of the lockdown.
That's a big area to search in that limited time.
6 wings, plus all the areas of the jail.
I had to write down every member of staff available to me and ensure there were enough to get the task done on time.
No pressure eh?
I've always said it and always will.
The staff at Frankland were professional, easy going and helpful.

We did that full lockdown search by 11.30 am.

Earlier I said that staff were referred to as " The Geordie Mafia" by ex Prisoners.

Complete nonsense. I'm not even a Geordie.

Yes, if an alarm bell went, the Cavalry came charging in droves.

Whatever happened, they had your back at all times.

Nearly everyone.

The only 2 times I recall where they didn't was the earlier mentioned attempted assault where the officer saw it but said he didn't .

Then there was the time I was driving to work and my car came off the road and smashed into a tree.

A colleague drove right past even though he witnessed it, got into work and said

" Dangerous drove off the road and hit a tree"

My colleagues asked if he'd stopped.

His reply

" Nah, I didn't want to be late for work"

My colleagues told me they were mortified by his actions.

Luckily, a Governor and another member of staff saw it and came to my aid and luckily I got out of the car uninjured.

Thank you Governor Fox and Brian.

Governor Fox took me to Durham hospital so I could get checked over.

Remember back to Whitemoor during the riot?

A prisoner had my back, yet here was a colleague that couldn't be arsed.

You can't get on with everyone.

But…

If I'd seen him crash, I'd have been straight out of my car to his aid.
Some people eh?

I've worked with some notables in my time. Neilsen , A certain massive prisoner who had a film made about him a few years ago, one of the Richardson gang,Charlie Kray etc… all have their own certain menace and notoriety about them.
I don't need to write much about these guys that you haven't already read or seen on screen.

Frankland welcomed the infamous Dr Shipman.
The first time I clapped eyes on him was to search him.
I saw this tiny 5ft odds ,bespectacled guy who looked like well, nothing.

Now The notorious one was a 6ft odd built like a brick shithouse kinda guy.
Shipman was the very opposite.
If I didn't know them from Adam as they say , I would've picked out Mr Notorious as a killer looking at the 2 of them.
At least with Mr Notorious, he actually appreciated humour when he wasn't fighting with staff or other Prisoners, and he'd never killed anyone.
Shipman was quiet and droll to say the least.
The one thing I did notice was his stare.
 He had "I'm a killer and I don't care "
written all over that stare.
2 of us searched him in the hospital wing.
We couldn't house him anywhere else as there may have been Prisoners families affected by his evil wrongdoings.
He had hardly anything in his cell. A few files, stationary and that was about it.
Very sparse , which made our job easier.

He wasn't popular but not altogether unpopular.
A lot of Prisoners would shout to him asking for advice on what the Prison Doctor should prescribe to them.
Shipman was the butt of certain jokes and he didn't like mine.
I can't even print mine as some may find it offensive like Shipman did.

A member of staff had asked him previous to my joke if he was a boxer.
"No I wasn't " he replied.
The staff member said
" Well, I heard you've got a lethal jab"
I found that funny.
Believe me my joke was far worse.

I had a famous London Gangster on Red Spur at Whitemoor.
He was in the opposite gang to the Krays in London. Now this guy was a superb artist. I watched him do a portrait for someone in his cell. I'm not joking when I say that the portrait was so lifelike.
He had some talent and was a pleasant enough guy to staff.

The massive Prisoner I mentioned was at Whitemoor and Frankland.
His notoriety is well known to everyone.
As aforementioned, you've all read about him or seen his film.
All I will say is that I remember him being on Frankland Segregation unit excercise yard one day.
Loads of prisoners were shouting
" Hey Charlie, remember me?"
He turned to me and said
" I don't fackin know any of these Mr D"
We both laughed at this.
He had a sense of humour.

I was working one day in Whitemoors Segregation Unit with a colleague called Ritchie.
Ritchie said to him
" Keep taking the beauty pills"
The reply was the usual " Fack off".
He tried telling us he was handsome.
I said " What about that moustache?, if I had a nose like that I'd never underline it"
He found this incredibly funny and gave out a loud laugh.
So instead of talking about his reputation, I'll leave it at that.

A lot of people wonder how Drugs get into Prison.
Our job on DST was to find them.
Drugs come in through Visits or Staff . It's as simple as that.
How? You may ask.
Simple answer, orifices, babies nappies and regurgitated.
Yep, regurgitated.
I was on duty in visits at Frankland when a female visitor began to choke. A Governor (Robson) sadly no longer with us, was right next to her when it happened.
He gave her the Heinrich manoeuvre.
As he did this balloons were coming out of her mouth.
Balloons packed with heroin.
One balloon bursting in her system and its lights out.
I grabbed the balloons she had regurgitated and the woman was rushed to hospital. The prisoner she was visiting was raging as he didn't get what he wanted.
Now some people are so scared that they will take risks.
Bearing in mind visitors go past a drug dog.
I was in the visits foyer with another DST colleague.
A woman came up to me and said
"Can you please pretend I've been caught?"
I asked her why?

" I don't want to traffic drugs into the prison"
She explained that she had been pressured from the outside to take in drugs to her partner.
I immediately radioed the orderly Officer.
She told me she had a lot of heroin on her person.
The orderly officer contacted the Police who dealt with her from there.
Turns out her life had been threatened.
I believe she got protection after that.

Drugs also come through through the post.
I remember working in Reception one day with a female colleague.
We put a pair of jeans through the x Ray machine that had been sent in through the post for a prisoner.
We could clearly see something wasn't right.
Somebody must have had patience beyond a saint.
They had unpicked the side stitching of the jeans put heroin into clingfilm all the way down both side seams and stitched the jeans up again.

The amount of drugs I've found in greetings cards in my day is unbelievable.
Happy Birthday please find enclosed some Drugs.

We had one prisoner at Frankland who's partner worked for a known Health store.
She'd obviously been packing things to send out and putting extra in his, and I don't mean health products.
When the products came in they looked legit. X Ray machines can be an asset in Jails.
I was near the end of my time in the Prison Service when Boss chairs came in .

A chair that detects mobiles secreted, prior to that it was gut instinct or a metal wand. A handheld detector.
I was wanding a prisoner once and his nether regions bleeped.
I got him to confess . He had 3 SIM cards under his foreskin.
He handed them over. Glad I had gloves on.

Mobile phones in clingfilm up their backsides was very common especially when first coming into the jail.
Drugs are a menace in the prison system.
Not only through prisoners being under the influence but also the debt prisoners can get into.
Debtors don't come off too well in Prison. I've seen some horrendous injuries due to drug debts.
The hassle it caused us as staff is off the scale.
One story I will go into later on in the book is a very sad one.

I mentioned Hooch earlier. Another absolute menace.
My time on DST I found 100s of Gallons of the stuff.
Stinking mouldy fermented fruit.
I had a prisoner tanked up on the stuff on G wing. He came out fighting , we had to restrain him as he was uncontrollable.
I think he thought he was superman. He took a bit of controlling and wouldn't feel any pain from our wrist locks due to being totally intoxicated.
His arms were flailing, his speech was incomprehensible.
It wrecks your brain that stuff.
I personally don't know how they can drink it.

Frankland ,as I said earlier has 6 wings.
4 of them were Vulnerable prisoner wings.
Don't think for one minute that F and G Wings were the most lively because their population were made up of Gangsters, terrorists and the like.

The amount of alarm bell incidents were higher down on the VP units.
The amount of fights, attacks and such incidents were commonplace on A, B,C and D wings.

A funny incident on D Wing once during an alarm bell was when the Prison service changed Uniform companies.
We had a new make of trousers.
Our trousers had a key pocket located on the right leg ,which was like a front pocket for our keys to keep them from prisoners sight.
Remember from earlier,some have photographic memories.
I got onto D wing ones landing. I remember the alarm was on the twos landing. I nearly got to the steps when THUD, I hit the deck.
My keys had popped out of my pocket as I was running to the alarm. My keychain wrapped around my right leg and bang, I was floored.
There were quite a few prisoners laughing and clapping at my misfortune.
I got up, took a bow and carried on up to the twos landing.
I thought the key pockets were smaller than usual.
I got up to the twos, there were about five prisoners fighting.
There was enough staff by then to quell this.

I recall only too well I was on B wing searching one afternoon.
The alarm bell went on B2 landing.
I rushed to the scene. A prisoner said
" over there Mr D" he pointed.
I got to where he had pointed. A prisoner had just attacked a female officer.
Two of us quickly restrained the prisoner. He was still in a rage.

This time a Prisoner had hit the Alarm bell when he saw the attack luckily.
It could have been worse.
It was an evil , cowardly attack and I'm sure the female officer still feels traumatised by this. I hope she's doing well now.

I remember on G wing a prisoner was shouting abuse at a female officer.
Another prisoner went straight up to him and started beating him for it.
Attacks on females in Max Security jails are infrequent but are looked upon by the majority other prisoners as cowardly .
It's like a Prison code with most as a No No.
A lot of the Alarms on the VP wings were for fighting.

During our searches with DST most weapons found were on the VP wings.
Mostly razor blades melted into toothbrushes. Usually double bladed so if it rips your face it's harder to see back, leaving one hell of a scar.
I've seen prisoners with the Chelsea smile where their mouths are ripped by blades.
I found 3 of these razor weapons in one cell.
The prisoner, who's cell I was searching had previously done a Kangaroo court in a previous prison and hung his cell mate.
If anyone knows the film " Stir Crazy" this prisoner looked like the bald huge guy from that.

He was raging that I found these weapons.
I obviously nicked him for it.
Two days later a member of staff said
"Come and see this"
He took me to that prisoners cell.
He'd scratched on his wall

" I'm going to kill screw Duncan"
This prisoner had issues.

Frankland had a DSPD open.
Dangerous and Severe Personality Disorder unit.
We had to search it.
I was up there with the DST.
I saw a prisoner hoovering the carpet on the unit. I noticed
there was no cable on the Hoover attached to a socket.
The prisoner was moving the hoover.
I said " you'd be better plugging that in"
He looked at me angrily and said
" it is fucking plugged in"
I pulled the cable out from the hoover and said " No it isnt"
He took the cable , put it back on the hoover, kept walking up
and down thinking he was hoovering.
The good thing about the unit is the staff working there got the
training they so needed.

A proud moment for me and the jail was we did a thing called
" Prison, me?, no way"
My colleague Billy, a female officer from Low Newton and
myself went around schools and colleges showing students the
harsh realities of prison life.
We had a mock wooden cell.
It was signed by the cast of bad girls.
We'd show them what prisoners wore, what happens inside
jails and weapons.
We'd tell them how they had to share a cell with another
prisoner and told them to imagine picking up their meal from
the servery to eat it, only to find their cell mate is on the toilet
with the runs and they have to sit and eat.

We did a week long roadshow in Stockton where students had to vote for best presentation. Others were Coastguard, Police, council and others.

We got over 90 percent of the vote ,thus winning a trophy which was displayed in the Jail.

Billy, the female colleague and I were a great team.

I have one word for Billy which he will never forget.

Billy, for you ,

"Amut"

Meanwhile I noticed that HMP Haverigg were advertising for staff.

I had considered Haverigg whilst at Whitemoor and was taken around the jail in 1998 by a former Whitemoor colleague.

At the time the circumstances weren't right.

I applied in 2006 and got the transfer.

On my last day ,I went to visit my old colleagues around the wings to say farewell.

Word got to G Wing that I was coming up.

I got on the wing where I was jumped by staff, thrown in the G2 chest freezer where they got a couple of prisoners to sit on it for a couple of minutes.

I got out shivering.

Thanks for the frosty send off lads n lasses.

I'm going to leave the Frankland part of the book here.

To all the staff I worked with during my time at Frankland, a massive ,massive Thank You.

You gave me some of the best times I had in the Service.

Times I won't forget.

The statements about the "Geordie Mafia" are so untrue. It was camaraderie and sticking together during the hard times where Teamwork really shone through.

You were always one collective team.

Chapter 4.

Haverigg.

Wonder when we're getting home?

So in 2006 I arrived in Cumbria to start at HMP Haverigg.
Haverigg is on the outskirts of the sleepy little town of Millom
on the Cumbrian coast, right on the edge of the beautiful
Western Lake District.
The scenery around the area is breathtaking to say the least.
Millom was a fairly quiet town , but I liked the look of the
place. It still had an olde worlde feeling about it. Old shop
fronts, victorian and Edwardian terraced houses.
As aforementioned, I'd been round the jail before in 1998.
It didn't look much different from back then.
My first morning consisted of being shown around the
different areas of the jail.
A lot different compared to Maximum Security jails. A lot
more open.
No corridors with a myriad of gates.
Haverigg was once an RAF camp, converted to a jail in the late
60s.
On entering there is an old propellor memorial statue to
commemorate this.

The prison grounds are quite vast in size.
Residential units, a wing, kitchen, education block, segregation
unit and workshops.

It is rumoured that HMP Slade from porridge is loosely based on Haverigg.

Certainly the pig farm bit on the programme.

Haverigg had to shut their pig farm during the bad outbreak of foot and mouth disease a few years ago.

My first thoughts on walking around were how much ground it is to cover for the amount of staff.

I was to be based on the induction wing.

A and B wings. These 2 wings are only separated by gates basically.

It was a temporary build that had been there for years.

Not so temporary.

I was introduced to the staff that were on duty and shown everything and everywhere on the wing. A Wing had 2 landings containing 60 cells.

B Wing was just a mirror image of A wing except B wing had a servery area.

The view of " Black Combe " a hill which is basically six feet short of a mountain could be clearly seen from the window on B2 landing was amazing.

The morning was done. Basically a tour.

On my first afternoon the wing senior officer said to me

" You're DST trained aren't you?"

To which I said I was.

" Could you search a couple of cells on B wing?"

I said I'd be delighted to. I loved searching.

I was searching with a female officer who had previously worked in a similar prison to me previously.

I expected to find nothing to be honest.

WRONG.

I had only been in the cell a few minutes when I came across a bladed weapon. The toothbrush style. The old favourite.
Followed by a container of hooch.
1st day on, first Haverigg nicking.

We did another cell. Nothing this time.
I decided to search a cleaning cupboard accessed by prisoners.
I picked up a pillowcase, looked inside,saw lots of material inside it.
On pulling the material out I found about 20 balaclavas made from prison t shirts, eyes and mouth cut out just like a balaclava.
I took them to the office to show the senior officer.
His words, " it gets cold here"
I'm sorry, but when I find something like that in a jail the word cold doesn't come to mind.
The words
"it's about to get hot in here "
are nearer the mark.
Shocking.
My first couple of weeks on the wing I found various weapons and things prisoners had in cell that they weren't meant to have.
I suppose ,that since I'd come from more secure enclosed jails that I expected to find more stuff.

From early on I could feel the atmosphere on the wing.
It wouldn't take much to tip it over the edge. It's that gut instinct again.
There had been the odd scuffle on the wing but there was a definite tension.
I, and other staff started putting Security Information Reports in.

I even wrote and highlighted in the wing log book that it was my belief that we were about to lose the wing.
Plus they had just placed a known troublemaker on B Wing.

About a couple of weeks later I was on evening duty.
It was a Wednesday evening. Canteen night.
Now normally because the wings are on lockdown for canteen distribution we would unlock one side of a spur to collect their weekly goodies including tobacco and other foodstuffs like pot noodles, chocolate, cola etc....
Before we unlocked the noise on the wing was unbelievable.
Doors being kicked, abuse being shouted at us and threats.
I said to the Senior officer
" If we unlock half of one landing we're asking for it"
There were only 3 of us.
He agreed with me. We started letting them out 2 at a time.
The first 2 we're fine.
Once they returned to the cell I opened the next cell.
He came at me ,so I had to use force to push him back into his cell.
The next 2 we're ok. Then we opened the next 2. One of them started kicking off so I put him back in his cell.
It went on like this on B2 landing till we reached the last cell on there and went onto the ones landing.
By this time the duty Governor came on the wing and asked why canteen wasn't finished.
I said to him
" Listen to the wing, we're getting abuse, threats and had to forcibly put some behind their doors"
He looked at me and said
" This isn't a Cat A prison you work in now"
My reply
" No, they wouldn't act like this in a Cat A Governor"

I then said
" we will lose this wing very soon"
He laughed at me and then went onto A wing which wasn't as loud.
That Governor knew I was right.

Same again on the ones landing,more screaming abuse. I reckon half of the ones landing got their canteen at their doors due to their behaviour.
You couldn't hear yourself think for the noise.

The next day I was a late shift.
The wing when I walked on was eerily quiet.
A female Senior Officer said
" What do you think Tony?"
I replied
"Open them up for association tonight and we will lose B Wing"

Apparently the tension on the wing was brought up at the Governors morning meeting by Wing Senior officers.
The Governors reply was
" You are managers, manage it"
Absolutely disgraceful comment.
Just shows you how uncaring Senior Management was in the place at that time.

They made us unlock for association.
Biggest mistake they made.

As soon as we unlocked A and B wing, alarm bell B Wing rang over the radio.
It was full scale Kick off.

Unfortunately one of my colleagues was stuck on B1 landing having a table football table constantly rammed at him. Finally he got off B1 through the gate which I unlocked and shut before B Wing prisoners got to it.

My colleagues hands were already swelling up like balloons. He had used his hands to protect himself from the constant ramming of the table against his body.

B Wing erupted.

The noise , the smoke the smashing and crashing.

It was worse than the C Wing riot at Whitemoor.

We witnessed one prisoner get a TV smashed over his head. He was in a bad way. Some prisoners had made balaclavas , like the ones I found that I was told were for cold weather. They put them on in order not to be identified but as I worked on B wing I knew who they were.

One shouted to me

" Wanna negotiate Mr Duncan?"

I replied " I don't negotiate with pieces of shit like you" I was so angry at this point.

They'd set fire to offices, ripped up files , smashed their cells, three beds onto the landing to try and make barriacades. There was water everywhere.

They tried ramming me with broom handles when I was at the gate. It was absolute chaos.

The ones that didn't really want to riot joined in.

60 prisoners running amok to cause as much damage as they could.

We managed to talk the young kid who was injured with the TV to edge his way to the gate.

When he did it a colleague quickly unlocked the gate ,and a colleague and I snatched at him to get him off B Wing.

We took a side of him each and dragged him quickly away from any more danger.

He was in a bad way. Blood pissing out of his head.
I had to stand and watch my place of work being torn apart.
I was raging inside.

A female Governor came on the wing.
" How are you ?"she said.
Bad timing.
" How am I? I'm fucking raging at all you managers, this is
your faults" I was more than angry at this point.
" You're all incompetent , one of my colleagues is going to
hospital, I told you this would happen, you didn't listen"
I remember my words like it was yesterday.

She was speechless. She walked away to the SOs office.
The rioting continued. B Wing was a complete mess,
unrecognisable.
Furniture, TVs, all sorts just strewn everywhere.

I'd only been at Haverigg 5 minutes.
The sign outside the prison says welcome to Haverigg.
I'd change that to Welcome to Hell.

The problem with Haveriggs location is it's at least an hour to
get to from the M6.
Mustering riot teams is a nightmare for North West prison staff
to get to.
The nearest jail was HMP Lancaster Castle which is a good
hour and a half away. Then there's Preston, Garth , Wymott etc
who have to muster staff as well to get to Haverigg.
Logistical nightmare.
Plus, they weren't on standby in case Haverigg kicked off.
This information should've been passed on a day ago, just in
case.

There wasn't enough staff at Haverigg alone to muster a team to take back B Wing.

Not all staff are C and R 3 trained which is the training you must complete to go into a prison riot.

Prisoners knew that there wouldn't be riot teams coming for quite some time so they could smash up even longer.

When the Teams finally mustered they took back B Wing easily without much of a fight back.

The next morning the staff were gathered for a debrief.

The Governor thanked the staff and said

" This was an unplanned spur of the moment act of concerted indiscipline"

Immediately I stood up and said

" Is that why I put Security information Reports in and also warned of this in the Wing log book 2 weeks ago?"

The Governor told me to keep calm.

"Calm, a member of staff is in hospital, B Wing is trashed, all of this could have been avoided. You ignored staffs warnings"

The Governor stammered and went onto something else.

I was raging.

There was 100s of thousands of pounds worth of damage, a staff member hurt.

All avoidable, management should have been listening to the troops on the ground. I wasn't the only one to put in SIRs or enter info into the log book. Other wing staff had put in info also.

There were reams of entries.

You can't see or feel it sat in an office.

It may be a business to them,but to us it was our bread and butter being out on them landings.

After the debrief we walked up to the wing. Our saving grace was A Wing all banged up the night before.

Imagine if they'd joined in?

A whole unit would've been destroyed.

We walked onto B Wing. The mess was indescribable. It looked like a landfill site.

The main perpetrators were taken out and shipped out to other jails.

The cleaners on the wing were unlocked as they volunteered to help in the clean up. Wellington boots and gloves had been supplied as there was so much water damage. There was electrical cabling ripped out, cells that were uninhabitable, fire damage, broken glass, smashed up games tables and just a pile of smashed furniture piled up as if it was coming to bonfire night.

All it needed was a Guy Fawkes on top.

B wing was well and truly Trashed.

Some of the head honchos from HMP headquarters came to see the damage.

We all mucked in.

By 4pm that day the debris was cleared up. The wing was looking like a wing again of sorts.

To be fair, the cleaners did an amazing job despite the abuse they were taking from prisoners who were banged up.

" Screw boy" was getting shouted at them. Insinuating that they were sucking up to us.

They, like us just wanted some kind of normality.

My colleague who was injured never came back.

I began to wish I was back at Frankland already.

There was a lot of unrest still on the wing .

Prisoners who had taken part in the rioting trying to get at prisoners who had helped clean up.

The words " Screw boy" were still being shouted at those that helped.

We had to restrain some of the ones who were mouthing off.

A lot of tension.

This has a knock on effect that reverberates through the whole jail.

There were incidents on Res 2 which was an open piece of land with 8 billets on it.

Res 2 was a nightmare at the best of times. It had Prisoners from all areas of the UK residing on it, but the biggest contingent were from Liverpool.

The Liverpool crew stuck together like glue. Mostly. But that's another story for later.

We knew they had the monopoly on R2 in the jail and kept a watchful eye on them.

They were involved with and in most cases ,EVERYTHING.

Most were young bits of kids from different areas of the city.

Streetwise, unafraid of anything and anyone.

One of them said to me once

"Wish I'd been on B Wing that night of the riot"

After the riot I noticed the level of violence on Res 2 increased.

Attacks on Prisoners was on the up.

R2 was very difficult to Police from a staff point of view. Too many places to hide.

As I said prior, we were lucky on Res 1 that A wing didn't erupt along with C wing that night but there were a few prisoners on A wing that were trying.

One was a lad from Preston. He got unlocked for his tea meal two nights after the riot and screamed

" Let's smash A wing"

Immediately I ran to him and with 2 other staff we restrained him,taking him straight back to his cell.
Other prisoners saw this and began kicking their doors.
I thought here we go again.
Luckily it didn't happen.
The lad from Preston was shouting
" Let's kill Mr Duncan"
I went to his cell with another member of staff and said
" One more threat like that you'll be taken to segregation"
He then went for me.
Two restraints in one evening. Same person.
We took him to "The Block"(Segregation).
Each day there seemed to be sporadic incidents. Little fights , abuse to staff following the riot.
Some prisoners,it seemed were hellbent on starting another one.
It took a couple of weeks for the wing to settle down properly.
It settled and things carried on.

Res 2 seemed to be heating up . Countless alarm bells going off.
Attempted assaults on staff and prisoners.
R2 was getting out of hand.
They were probably jealous of B Wings recent riot.
By this time it was near the Christmas of 2006.
I did a hooch purge on R2 and Res 3 with the Security department. We found gallons of the stuff. A great time to purge for Hooch.
Christmas is a time when prisons can get a bit edgy and if a prison would get edgy Haverigg was a good bet.

Sure enough. New Year's Eve 2006 it went pear shaped.

We were doing feeding in the main dining hall. A massive movement of prisoners from R2 , R3 , R4 and programmes group all coming to the hall at once.

I was stood down at R3 gate with Oscar 1.

I spotted a load of prisoners making a run for the gate.

It was like a herd of elephants charging toward us. Just as they got nearer I managed to close the gate on them.

They were screaming at me banging the gates shouting

" we will get you Duncan"

I just laughed and said

" I know all your names.

I nicked about 15 Prisoners at that gate.

Our job then was to get them all back on their own units and locked up.

Not an easy task with around 200 Prisoners running around.

The call came over the radio from Oscar 1

" All available staff to the dining hall"

Every member of staff in Haverigg got to the dining hall. We were restraining prisoners, getting them locked up, going back, restraining more then back again.

It was Hell.

Haverigg was Hell.

The saying " Winter of Discontent" was ringing true.

It was around 10pm when we finally got Roll correct and staff could go home.

I'd been on duty since 07.30 that day.

Happy New Year eh?

I got home to see the bells at least.

Praying 2007 would be better at work as I sat with my single malt.

I was off New Year's Day and returned on January 2nd 2007.
A new year, a new start.

I'd been at Haverigg 3 months.

I walked up to the wing to the shout of a Mancunian voice.

" Mr Mckays coming on the wing"

It was to alert other Prisoners to hide stuff . I heard a lot of toilets flushing.

A sign that hooch was being disposed of in case they got a search.

They gave me that nickname from Fulton Mckays role in porridge.

I asked the prisoner who had shouted it.

He told me that I had the same harshness as Mr McKay.

I told him I'd rather be a McKay than a Barraclough.

He was the softer easier going Prison Officer in the series.

He shook my hand and said

" Happy New year Mr McKay"

I took this as a compliment.

It's funny but Prisoners did come to me a lot as they got a straight answer.

One said to me

" Why do you always say no?"

I told him that I can come back on a No but I can't come back on a yes.

" What do you mean?"

I told him that if he asks me for something and I say no,but later on I can help it's turned a no into a yes . But if I automatically say yes, and then I can't help, there's no way back on that.

On the day I returned in 2007 the morning went smoothly. We unlocked after lunch. One prisoner on B1 had barricaded in his cell. Spy hole covered up and his window at the rear of his cell was covered with a towel.

At first he wouldn't speak to staff.

I'd been off the wing for some reason and came onto B1.

It was a young Geordie lad. I went to his cell door and said I'd speak to him if he removed the tissue he had covering his spy hole.

Straight away he said

" I'll speak to you only Mr Duncan"

I told him I wasn't speaking to him behind a door and asked him to remove the barricade.

At first he refused.

I explained that it's far easier to talk with the door open instead of me having to shout through a metal door and that other prisoners could hear if I have to shout.

He took the barricade away.

I told him I was going to open his door and come in.

I cracked the door open and shot the safety bolt so as I couldn't get locked in the cell.

I asked what was wrong.

He showed me multiple cuts he'd done on his arms , legs and body.

I asked for all his blades before I would sit and talk to him.

I put gloves on as he handed me quite a few blades wrapped in tissue.

I passed them to a colleague to dispose of them safely.

I sat with the lad for about 30 minutes listening as to why he self harmed.

It was family reasons.

I told him he'd probably be put on a constant watch for his own safety.

He was ok with this.

He said to me near the end of the conversation

" A lot of cons think you're a bastard but you're not really, you're a good Officer that takes no shit"

2 compliments in one day.

He was put on a constant watch which started a spate of this.
If memory serves me well he was one of 5 on B wing in the
first week of January to be on a watch of some sort.
Constant means just that.
Watched 24/7. There has to be an officer at the cell door Sat
watching.
For staff who love overtime it's a great thing.
I'm sure we hit double figures by the end of January between
A and B wings.
I'm sure a lot of it was through bullying by other Prisoners but
no one would tell us.
If we suspected or were told that a prisoner was bullying we
put them on an anti bullying monitoring form where the
individuals were very closely monitored.
All these forms like Self harm forms and anti bullying forms
were taken wherever the Prisoner went eg Workshops and
education.

Early on in 2007, if I remember it was March or April I got
wind that B Wing Prisoners were planning to riot again.
I made it my mission to avoid this so one afternoon I decided
to unlock all of them and directed them to the TV room on B
Wing.
I sat with them and told them on no certain terms would I have
another riot on my wing.
I had A4 sheets of paper and individually asked them what
their issues were.
I wrote them all down Prisoner by prisoner.
I warned them that I wouldn't tolerate another riot and I would
not tolerate any violence if they did riot ,toward the female
staff on the wing, of which there were a few.
My tactic worked. B Wing did not riot again.

We had another form of which I was adept at.
It was called a "Formal Warning form"
It was like 2 strikes and out.
Prisoners on the wings were on 3 levels.
Incentive based levels.

Enhanced,where they had TVs in cell and other privelidges.
Standard level where they had TVs but less privelidges.
Basic Level where they had no TVs and no privelidges.
It was a good system to try and keep the wing in order.
So if a prisoner got 2 formal warnings for not adhering to
Wing rules,they'd get a board with the Senior officer on the
wing.
If it was decided the warnings stuck they were downgraded.
For example, if a Prisoner on Enhanced got 2 warnings and
they stuck, he'd be downgraded to Standard and lose certain
privelidges.
An example of wing rules was going to prisoners cell doors
when they're not supposed to, or improper use of their cell call
button.
To give you an idea of how adept I was with this system here's
a quote from an old colleague of mine ,Terry.

"Tony,it was funny as fuck ,unless you were on the Evening
Duty,as after you'd gone.
Fucking more lights than Blackpool"

Improper use of cell call buttons they were for Emergencies
only. Misuse of them annoyed me as they were normally for
things like,
" Can you pass this newspaper to the cell next door please
boss?"
I made a rule of that on my first set of nights at Haverigg.

I took the newspaper through the gap in the door, checked it for contraband,put it outside the next cell door and said
" He can get it on unlock tomorrow, I stopped being a Paper boy when I was 15"
Passing papers is not an emergency.
I always answered cell call buttons promptly in case it was something serious or genuine.
Anything non serious it was a formal warning form issued.
If not, you'd be run off your feet all night.
I never got many improper use of button much after that.

We had some laughs on Res 1 though.
One time a colleague of mine was going to a fancy dress party . She was going as a punk.
I'd been in a Punk/ Gothy type of band a few years earlier so I brought her in some zipped red tartan punk trousers I still had.
My plan was to unlock after lunch wearing said trousers for a laugh for prisoners.
Sadly a female Governor came on the wing and spoiled the fun.
I had to dart to a medical room to put my uniform trousers back on. She wouldn't have seen the funny side of it.

Here's a quote from Mark, my old colleague and tag team partner.

"When you had your tartan pants on and a female Governor come onto the wing and you were trying to change them in A Wing medical waiting room"

We rarely got Governor visits. Trust it to be when I was going to use a bit of humour.

Talking of trousers. We had a Prisoner who, let's say wasn't the cleanest. In fact one of the dirtiest I'd ever come across. All he wore was prison issue clothing which included the standard grey track suit bottoms which were too big for him. He refused to get smaller ones as hard as we tried.
One lunchtime on B1 he went for his dinner. On walking back to his cell his tracksuit bottoms came down to his ankles. He had no boxer shorts on.
He came walking up to me starkers from the waist down holding his dinner, looked at me and said
" Can you pull me Kegs up boss"
Well I burst as did the whole wing as I leant down to pull up the trackies.
He then went to his cell, put his meal down the toilet and started washing his plate and plastic cutlery in his toilet bowl.

A quote from Mark.

"Ha ha plenty of memories of you Turbo , pull my kegs up boss"

I got the nickname " Turbo" from Mark due to partly my initials TD, Turbo Diesel, and partly from the way I raced to General alarms in the jail.
I'd speed off as quickly as I could.
I was fit back then.

Mark and I always seemed to be on duty together when something went off.
We seemed to be the wings tag team.
I recall one evening duty when 3 prisoners were fighting each other on B Wing. We were the only 2 staff on the landing at the time. Mark hit the alarm bell but by the time staff

responded we had the 3 Prisoners in a crumpled heap with us on top of them.

One afternoon I gave a prisoner a second formal warning.
He got his award which was down from standard to basic.
He walked away from his board onto the wing.
CRASH, furniture started flying at myself and Mark.
Chairs the lot. We were like Laurel and Hardy dodging this, forward, backwards, sideways. Finally we got to him and restrained him.
He apologised later.

By this time a colleague and his partner had transferred to Haverigg from Whitemoor. He came to Res 1 to work.
He worked in the same way I did. No nonsense.
It wasn't long before this disgruntled prisoners and accusations started flying at us.
Prisoners didn't like the way we ran A and B wings.
Yes, it's a Category C jail, yes it's less restricted ,but Prison rules are prison wide.
Flout them and you get placed on report. Simple as that.

Prisoners know full well that they don't get placed on report or warnings for no reason.
The nicking sheets were getting dished out daily as well as formal warnings and A wing and B wings prisoners got disgruntled.
I'd been on a fortnights leave in Scotland.
On my return to work I had a note on my keys. Report to the Governors office at 1.45 that day.
I went along the admin corridor where I was met by a member of the Prison Officers Association.
I asked what was going on, I hadn't stepped out of line at all.
I was always professional at my job.

He said" The Governor is going to suspend you"
I asked why?
He replied " Not even I know"
We went in.
There was the number 1 Governor, Deputy Governor and the Governors secretary taking notes.
In front of me was a tape recorder which the Governor duly switched on. The first of 2 times I'd have to do a taped interview.
The Governor read out his spiel regarding taped interviews and proceeded.
" on the 15th February 2007, you entered cell B2-30 and assaulted Prisoner .... By repeatedly punching him in the face"
Immediately I said
" Is that right Governor?" And smiled.
He told me this was what the prisoner had alleged.
" I put it to you Governor that you are incompetent" I replied.
He stuttered, " I beg your pardon , this is a serious allegation"
Again I smiled and wanted to laugh.
I asked the Governor if he'd checked the landing cameras from that time and date.
" No" was his reply.
I then said " Did you check Staffs leave at that time and date?"
Again I got a no.
I laughed this time and being one who speaks his mind I said
" I'd need to be stretch fucking Armstrong then Governor to hit him that day, I was in Falkirk"

At that , his face went bright red, he looked at the Deputy Governor and his secretary, suspended the interview, stopped the tape and sat quietly for a few moments.
He then asked to speak to me outside the office.

I took my POA colleague with me.

The Governor apologised to me.

He had not done his homework on this.

This was not my last dealing with the Number one Governor.

The same prisoner also accused my colleague who had came from Whitemoor of the same thing.

It was all fabricated bull.

Turns out, I found out from another Prisoner,that the accusing Prisoner had been punching himself, hitting his head off his cell wall etc to bruise himself and make it look like he'd been assaulted.

Some Governors at the jail were superb. Some were just business managers walking about with blinkered eyes.

One day I was going into the main Prison through an electronic gate. I saw a Governor approaching. I did what I always did and waited at the gate till the Governor approached ,it's basic Security procedure in any jail.

Never leave a gate open and unattended.

This Governor got to the gate and said,

" You could've left it, you're not at Frankland now" I laughed and said

"Pity I'm not"

The following week someone left the gate open.

I was coming out of the Security office. I spotted a Prisoner hiding behind a car that was parked inside the prison near the big main gate. I apprehended him.

He was a hairsbreadth away from that gate opening ,and his freedom.

My next taped interview was to do with the B Wing riots.

There were 3 Governors came from other Prisons as independent interviewers,investigating the riot from my perspective.

Here was my chance to get the truth out there.

I sat in a room with a Governor on B Wing.

The first thing he asked was

" Did you think there would be a riot on B Wing or A Wing?"

I replied

" B Wing for certain, I could feel it, I'd had this feeling before"

He then said

" Did you put in SIRs?"

I told him I had and also logged my info in the wing log book.

He then said

" Is the log book here? if so I need to photocopy your entry and any subsequent entries"

I knew where he was going with this.

As far as he was aware there was no information leading up to the riot.

Now he knew there was.

My info was enough to prove there was intelligence to suggest an up and coming riot.

He then asked what happened during the riots.

I told him everything I knew from build up to when I left the prison that night.

The whole truth,and how my information was laughed off and ignored.

We then went to the centre office, took the log book upstairs and photocopied my entries and other staff entries pertaining to the riot.

The Governor I spoke to was very pleased with all I had told him and the evidence I'd presented to him.

My last story from being on B Wing was on nightshift prior to me leaving the wing.

I was Oscar 2. Basically 2nd in charge of the jail. It was Christmas Eve.

The Operational support Grades did the wings on night state at Haverigg. Oscar 1 is in charge of the Prison during night state. This time Chris Kennedy was Oscar 1.

Although It was The night before Christmas, all was calm, all was quiet.

We decided to go around the Wings to visit the staff on duty. Whilst we were on Programmes we got a call on the radio to ring the control room.

Chris rang control.

We were told that there was movement heading toward R4s fence line. We quickly made our way to R4.

We alerted the OSG on R4 to come with us. We stayed very quiet.

All of a sudden black bin bags came flying over the fence. There were 4 in total.

We shouted

" Merry Christmas from the Haverigg staff" loud enough so the intruders could hear us. They ran off into the distance.

We took the bags to the control room.

All 4 bags were brimmed full of mobile phones and blocks of cannabis.

There was some amount in that haul.

Daylight came.

Christmas Day.

Over the radio the Haverigg dog handler who had been patrolling the fence said

" Merry Christmas, there's a full bag of KFC and cola stuck to the fence that didn't quite make the throw over last night"

We were in fits of giggles.

The cheeky sods had even tried to throw KFC buckets over. The lengths that people go to eh?

Sadly. Not long after I left the service , Oscar 1, Chris Kennedy passed away.
As I know your love for "Joy Division"was as big as mine Chris…
" Don't walk away, in Silence".
Rest in peace mate.

I left B Wing to go onto the Security Department, probably a lot to do with my searching. The Security Governor had approached me and asked if I'd like to join the team.
Immediately on joining they asked me to do some intelligence led searches.
One was for a phone.
I got to the guys cell with a colleague.
Instantly you could see he was nervous.
I asked the usual.
"Is there anything in this cell that there shouldn't be?"
Nervously he said no.
I said
" There is, isn't there?"
"No boss, honest"
I said I had reason to believe there was.
He then panicked and started to make a run for his door. We stopped him, he raised his hand to punch me.
He failed. My colleague and I restrained him and raised another member of staff and we searched him under restraint.
Only to find a mobile phone in his trousers.
After that ,we searched inside a billet on Res 3. Result was 2 mobile phones, gallons of hooch and a bag of yeast.

On returning to Security with our finds I knew I was going to get a lot of Searching tasks.

That was 3 mobiles in the space of one hour.

Mobile phones at that time were at a premium. A tenner cheap phone was worth around £100 in jail to a prisoner.

One with a camera was at least £200.

Haverigg is right on the coast of Cumbria. Easy access, as all there is to get to it is sand dunes and a field.

On an evening duty on Security we regularly patrolled the beach area in a land rover looking out for potential throw overs. This is where prisoners set up their mates on the outside to come to Haverigg, get near to the fence and throw stuff over for prisoners to collect.

Remember the Christmas Eve story earlier?

So the searching purges began on the wings.

Res 3 was a favourite.

The billets had an attic space. Now to the naked eye you wouldn't think they'd been tampered with but me being me I was always suspicious.

I was on one billet searching, if memory serves me well it was E4.

I decided to check the attic hatch. Sure enough it had been tampered with.

I got up into E4 roof space.

It was like a brewery up there. There must have been over 20 gallons of hooch right at the start of the roof space. I radioed the Security Senior Officer and asked him to report to E4.

He came up to the roof space and in his Sunderland accent said " fuck me marra, that's enough for a staff Christmas party"

Time to check all the roof spaces on R3 before word got round.

We stopped prisoners from moving around the billets and did all the roof spaces of all R3 billets.

You might as well have called it "R3 Distillery" you'd have needed a lorry to move the amount we found.

I recall finding metal weapons, makeshift screwdrivers and SIM cards in the roof spaces.

I decided to check everywhere I could on the billets the next day. Not cells, just areas. More mobiles, more makeshift tools and more weapons.

I was getting abuse shouted at me from billets. They don't like it when you undo their good work.

Myself and my colleague Rob were now public enemy number one at Haverigg.

We were finding all the things that they'd took time to hide. Remember, prisoners have 24 hours a day to make things and think of places they can hide them.

It's like a game. They hide stuff, we seek it.

One morning I took a walk around the grounds. I was near R3. I noticed a tennis ball. You might not think anything of it, but it sitting in Prison grounds is unusual to Prison Officers.

I radioed Billy,the Senior Officer as I didn't have the key to access the area.

He came along and we got the said tennis ball. On picking it up I noticed it had a split in it.

There was something inside it.

We took it back to the Security office.

It was packed with brown powder.

We got the police in to take it away.

Turns out it was £40,000 worth of Heroin.

In time I searched all the residential units and found phones, hooch and weapons in abundance.

One in particular was a matchstick, wooden , handmade Grandfather clock.

Prisoners make a lot of things from matchsticks.

I had noticed it moved around different cells. I had checked it to see if there were secret compartments in it. I found nothing.

Eventually more through curiosity , I took it to get X-rayed.

Now on this clock it had 4 feet on it. The clock was around 10 inches high.

On x- raying the clock I could see strips of metal in it.

We took it apart.

All 4 feet were double razor bladed.

4 weapons in one matchstick clock.

Ingenious to be honest.

Haverigg was a haven for searchers.

I went on R2 one day doing area searches. At each end of the billets was a carpeted area. I unscrewed the carpets.

My god there were literally 100s of weapons on R2 under the said carpets of all varieties.

Some of them deadly.

Some haul that day.

The next day I went on R2 in the evening where a hail of stones came flying over one of the billets at me.

Luckily none hit me, but we're obviously intended for me.

A few days later I was on R3 and a prisoner who hailed from Manchester started hurling abuse at me.

Now, it was right outside E7 billet which I nicknamed " Anfield Row"

It was full of Liverpudlians.

E7 ,I had a good relationship with. I got on with all the Prisoners on that billet.

The Prisoner came up to me face to face still hurling abuse.

Another colleague had joined me.

I said to the Prisoner

" Go and bang up"

He refused. At this time all I heard from E7 was

" Deck him Mr D" in a Scouse voice.

The prisoner refused a direct order to go to his cell.

Faced with no choice we restrained him to the sounds of clapping , cheering and " Yesssss Mr D" coming from E7.

Years later whilst living in Liverpool I bumped into an ex prisoner from E7 and he reminded me of this incident and said " All us Scousers loved you on that billet, you were a fair screw".

Not long after this incident a bucket of urine and faeces was being prepared for me to be potted.

" Potted" is where the contents of a bucket, usually as described above would be thrown over you.

A prominent Liverpool prisoner came to me.

I had known him since my Whitemoor days.

He said " I've sorted it Mr D"

I replied " Sorted what?"

He then told me that the Manchester contingent had made up a bucket to pot me due to that incident a few days ago.

He told me that he'd approached some of the Manchester lads and said if that bucket goes over Mr Duncan you will all get done over.

He watched them dispose of the bucket.

I know quite a few staff who have had this. It's a disgusting thing to do to anyone and the tests you have to go through for disease is a long agonising wait. AIDS, hepatitis etc….

One find at Haverigg was linked to a sad story.

On R2 a prisoner had taken his own life.

When any prisoner does this it's upsetting for staff and some other Prisoners

I knew the prisoner from R1 on induction.

He was a very quiet lad and never bothered anyone.

No one knew why he had done this.

Two days later a Prisoner came to me in confidence.

" I know why that prisoner took his own life"

I asked "Why?"

The prisoner who had passed away had been sharing a cell.

His cell mate got out on early release. When he left the jail he had drug debts in the region of £1000.

He never paid up.

The prisoners he owed money to then went to the cell , now only occupied by the quiet guy.

Although the debt had nothing to do with him the other prisoners put the debt on the quiet guy and apparently doubled it to £2000.

Obviously the prisoner couldn't afford it but was held at knifepoint with a prison made combat styled knife.

As a result , the threatened prisoner committed suicide.

I asked the prisoner that had came to me with all this info, "Where is the knife and who threatened him?".

He told me he couldn't give names but said,

" The knife isn't in the billets, it's outside of them"

We began conducting searches of R2. Nothing.

We did the whole of the grounds, billets etc…

The next lunchtime myself and my colleague Rob got a set of ladders from the works department.

Bingo.

Rob retrieved the knife from the guttering on D5 billet if I remember rightly.

This thing was lethal. It was so sharp it cut through paper like butter. It was pointed and had the ripping part cut in it.
It was quite a professional job.

I'm so glad we got it as how many more people had been threatened or were going to be threatened by this lethal piece of kit?
It was rumoured who had threatened the Prisoner with it but you can't go on rumour.
We had a suspicion who had made it.
Probably thrown from a workshop window into the prison grounds, picked up by a litter picker, put in his black rubbish bag then distributed through a cell window to the person who wanted it made.
Job done.

Less than a week later I found the template for it in the woodwork workshop along with another template for a knife.
Who's to say the next one made wasn't intended for staff?

Another incident that sticks in my mind whilst working on Security.
Two Prisoners came back into R2 from visits.
They were mouthing off to others that they had drugs secreted up their rectum.
Other Prisoners decided that they wanted the drugs
Whilst the 2 prisoners were sat in a cell they were jumped.
Allegedly by the Scouse contingent on R2.
Some Prisoners held them down whilst other prisoners dug into their rectums with plastic spoons, using the handle end of the spoons,desperate to take the drugs off them.
The 2 prisoners were rushed to hospital with masses of blood pouring from their backsides.
Turns out they had no drugs on their person at all.

The Liverpool prisoners ,as a rule got on ok, but one day all hell broke lose.

Croxteth and Norris Green in Liverpool are 2 housing schemes which are separated by a road.

They are sworn enemies.

It was feeding time in the dinner hall.

The two gangs decided to have it out with each other.

There were bodies piling into each other, punches thrown, prisoners being decked and stamped on.

The alarm bell was pressed,

" All available staff to the dining hall,draw your batons, I repeat, draw your batons"

We bombed it to the dining hall and waded in to quell the incident. They kept fighting.

The major concern was it was becoming every man for himself as others had started to join in.

One kid was lying bleeding on the floor, prisoners with burst noses, cut eyes etc… bloodbath.

One hell of a brawl.

Finally we took control of it and calmed it down.

I'd never had to use my baton in the service till that moment.

In 2008 I was approached by the Governor to appear in a week long series that BBC Northwest Tonight were doing called " Inside Haverigg"

I agreed to do this and asked him what he wanted to show on the slot I had.

" Show some of the weapons"he said.

So I did.

I showed the combat knife and various other gruesome weapons found at Haverigg.

I also said on the programme,

" These are some of the worst weapons I've come across in all my years in the service"

When it got televised the Director general of the prison service got in touch with the Number one Governor and was raging that I had said this.

Doesn't the truth hurt?

Now after my slot was shown on the programme the number one Governor was interviewed live by Gordon Burns the TV presenter.

The first question he asked was

" Do you think Haverigg is a safe Environment?"

The Governor replied

" Yes I believe it is"

Gordon Burns then said,

" I've just seen the weapons that the officer showed us there, I wouldn't call that safe, would you?".

The Governor was visibly lost for words.

Haverigg was not a safe Environment.

I started teaching Search Techniques for staff ,where I'd show staff where to look when searching and also how to properly search areas like Workshops etc. giving them tips on what to look out for and how to search methodically.

This was a popular class with staff.

I also took Security awareness sessions for new staff to the jail.

Key safety, personal safety etc..

I enjoyed the teaching side of the job immensely.

I should have went into teaching at the end of my career.

In 2008 on 29th August,The POA called on its members to take industrial action over pay conditions.

This was a totally illegal strike but enough was enough.

Our pay hadn't been in line with inflation. So we took to the outside of the gates at 7am and took the industrial action.

An action we could have legally been jailed for.

A policeman who was at our picket said and I quote.

" Who'd lock prisoners up if you guys were Jailed?"

It was funny though having to watch Managers working.

Shortly after this I became a trade Union Rep for the POA.

It wasn't too long before I'd be face to face with the Governor again.

The prisoners on A and B wings had put in complaints that by the time the food had been brought up on the heated trolleys from the kitchen it was cold.

Especially the chips.

When the food trolleys were unloaded the food was then put on a hot plate.

There's no way that food was cold.

Anyway, the word got round that the Governor was going to install deep fat fryers on the wings.

I was enraged and asked the other POA committee members to hold a meeting with the Governor.

A meeting was held.

I put it to the Governor that there were enough weapons on the wings without adding another.

He said about the complaints he'd received.

I said " I'd rather have complaints than a fatality"

He didn't seem bothered.

I reminded him of the incident back in 1995 where my colleague had hot fat thrown over him and subsequently took his own life due to this.

I thought the matter was over and done with.

I addressed the staff members who were in the POA of this and told them of my disgust that the Governor had suggested this.

Some of the staff had worked with and were friends with my former Whitemoor colleague and were as enraged as I was.
The implications of installing these were numerous.
We also informed the cleaners on the wing who served the food.
They were none too pleased either.

Picture the scene.
Prisoners coming to get fed.
One prisoner doesn't get on with another one or a particular member of staff.
He comes to the servery, sees the bubbling boiling fat and decides to jump into the servery itself.
Gets a container, puts the fat in it and launches it at someone.
The effect of this is devastating as I well know.

I went on leave for a week.
On my return a Prisoner , who was a cleaner on the wing said to me,
" Look at this Mr D?"
He led me to the servery.
There in front of me was an industrial deep fat fryer.
I was horrified.

The Governor in 1995 was a Catering Principal Officer when cooking oil was banned from wings following the incident at Whitemoor.
He knew damn well what it did in the wrong hands.
How could he do this?
The Prisoner then said,
" Someone damaged it, it doesn't work"

Although vandalism in Prison is the very thing we try to stop, I wasn't displeased that this god awful Weapon was out of use.

The Prisoner then told me that the Governor found out it was damaged.
The prisoner then said,

" The Governor asked us if Mr Duncan had told us to damage it"

I was absolutely raging at this.
I thought the matter was over. I didn't even know it had been put there let alone ask prisoners to damage it.

That year, I joined the Riot team at Haverigg. I was asked by the Security Senior officer, so off I went to Doncaster to do the training.
The training is brutal, as it should be.
Very very lifelike. You are put into riot situations that you would confront during indiscipline scenarios.
Fire, debris thrown at you, prisoners (Played by instructors)charging at you with varying weapons and then taking a wing back.
Great fun.
When I was doing this course there were some students from a local college observing us taking a wing back.
They were visibly shocked at the force of violence used during our training.
Nice having filing cabinets, blocks of wood, anything that could be thrown or used on you.
At one point I had to endure countless batterings on my shield by a prisoner attacking me with a broom handle.
Your arms start to ache , your eyes filled with sweat due to wearing a helmet,but in your head you think.
If I let go, I'm getting this broom handle rammed in my face.

Survival mode, Self preservation and Teamwork from those around you kick in.

You starting using Mind over matter.

And that's just the training.

Imagine the real thing?

The reason I named this chapter

" Wonder when we're getting home?"

Is due to the amount of Prisoners at Haverigg who got onto roofs at the jail.

Prisoners if agile enough could get onto the billet roof, the kitchen roof, in fact just about any roof in the jail.

And they did just that.

This involves any C and R 3 (Riot team) staff, negotiators, generally it disrupts the whole jail. You basically have to lock it down. Then you had to contact the Tactical unit as they were trained at working at height.

Prisoners go up on the roof for varying reasons. Debt, threats, wanting a move from the jail etc..

Roof climbers were abundant and usually it was at teatime or at lock up.

The evening ones were the worst.

I think every night we were waiting for control room to announce,

" All stations we have one on the kitchen roof"

As soon as it was called we had to go and get our PPE.

Helmets, overalls, knee and arm pads, boots and shields.

We mustered at the area and kept out of sight whilst the negotiator dealt with whoever was on the roof. Sometimes one prisoner, I have seen 3 up there before.

We used to pray for rain as it could sometimes be your friend and bring them down quicker.

I've seen these incidents last all night and into the next day.
I remember one rooftop lasting from teatime until 08.30 the
next day. We had to stay as C and R teams had to take the
prisoners to the segregation unit once they'd come down.
I'd always say,
" Wonder when we're getting home?".

An incident on R2 one evening, 4 prisoners barricaded in a
cell.
We, as a riot team got called out to it.
Negotiating wasn't working.
Eventually I went outside to the back of the cell.
I knew all 4 of them.
I said " Right guys, what's going on?".
They told me they were unhappy being at Haverigg.
I asked if they'd tried putting in for a transfer. Allegedly they
had, or so they told me.
I said " Guys, take down the barricade , as if we crack your
door open about 30 staff will storm the cell and you will get
hurt"
At first they said no, but after a bit more convincing I managed
to get them to agree.
I went into the billet and said to the teams they were coming
out.
I'd talked them into it.
They removed whatever they'd used to stop us gaining entry
and one by one they surrendered to the teams.
I admit I'm no negotiator like my father was, but sometimes
the way you deal with people does work.
I got praise for the way I handled the incident.

We had another cell barricade on A wing one night.
5 of them.

Our teams gathered.
Swarms of them.
They refused ,despite being asked on a few occasions to come out of the cell.

The door cracked open.
There was just a stream of blue helmets. Once the door is cracked there is no going back for prisoners. There were bodies everywhere, falling over each other. The prisoners tried fighting back. One tried head butting an Officer, I mean imagine trying when he has a helmet on with a visor.
It's laughable.
Fruitless trying.

There were screams, not from us, crashing ,banging, thudding. I got hold of one and dragged him out of the cell. 2 other staff got control of his arms , I took his head and we took him to the segregation unit under restraint, behind us ,the other 4 were also taken under restraint.
It took less than 5 minutes for us to take all 5 of them.
There is no point trying to fight teams of riot trained prison officers.
It's a no win situation.
The Governor who was observing admitted he'd never seen a riot team go through a cell as quickly in his whole career.

Can I just say, any Control and restraint used at any time is a last resort.
None of wanted to use it but at times we had to.
I want to make this very clear to readers.
If it wasn't justified , it wasn't used.

I've worked in teams before in the job but Haverigg C and R 3 team were nothing short of brilliant.

Professional ,but brilliant.

After this incident a couple of weeks later, I went into a cell that a Prisoner had smashed up.
We were in a 3 man team.
Toilet, sink, radiator off the wall . The cell was a mess and swimming with water which was brown and dirty.
I asked to him to face the wall with his hands behind his back. He complied.
I was number one officer.
Number one controls the head. It's like an arrow formation.
Number 1- head, 2s and 3s take the arms.
Number one has the shield.
The prisoner was stood facing the wall. We advanced quite quickly but I slipped.
I fell and smashed my back into the radiator. Right into the base of my back.
The prisoner turned around, I remember it vividly
" Are you ok Mr Duncan?" He said. He looked concerned to be honest.
The number one and number two in my team picked me up.
" You should go to the hospital Mr D" the prisoner said.
He was more concerned than I was.
He came forward and said,
" Take me to the block and get Mr Duncan to hospital"
I didn't go.
I just got up and got on with it.

All I had was a red mark on my lower back. Little did I know what damage I'd done.
 About a month later I started to get pain so excruciating that I was falling to the ground. I was getting pain akin to sciatica. I thought that's what it was.

I got to the point that I had to roll out of bed.
I couldn't go to work like that.
Imagine if id been on a landing or wherever in a jail and I just dropped.
Prisoners could take my keys, start on me, I mean, I wasn't the most popular officer at Haverigg.
All the things id found, all the cell take outs i'd done. I would've been a sitting duck.
This was August 2010.
I had to go off, not just for my safety but for Staff , prison and prisoner safety also.
I'd moved to The Wirral near Liverpool by this time .
In the October I felt pressured into going back.
Management were hassling me.
I went back even though I knew I wasn't right.

On my return I went to R2 office as I was going onto R2 to work.
My morning was awful. I didn't know if I was going to collapse or not.
I got asked to go and see the number one Governor.
A newer number one ,who I thought would have had more compassion.
No, they're all the same.
He asked me how I was.
I replied" Agony but you pressured me into coming back"
He said " aww but it's your back, you can't see injuries in your back so it's hard to tell if someone is making it up"

I thought , You bastard and came out with it.
"Did you get a doctorate from Kellogg's Cornflakes?"
He replied " What?"

I said " I'm walking out of this jail right now and going to my GP to get an MRI scan"
" You can't do that" he said.
" Watch Me" I replied.
With that I went straight to the gate, handed in my keys.
Never to return.

I went straight to my GP and asked if I could have an MRI.
He got me an appointment at a hospital on the Wirral.
I had my scan a week later.
Less than two weeks after the scan I got the results.
It read like war and peace the damage that the fall had caused.
I got a copy of the results of the scan to give to the Governor.
In the meantime I had a home visit from a female Governor.
The best Governor we had in the jail.
She read the scan report. I remember her words.
" Oh my God Tony, my partner came off his motorbike and this report is the same as his"
So my injuries were the equivalent of a motorcycle accident.

The MRI showed that bits of bone and disc had broken and were lodging in my spinal column, thus causing me to fall.
Even a specialist at Liverpool hospital told me that if he operated on me there was a big chance he'd damage my bladder or bowel and advised against operating.
Answer that one Mr Number one Governor.

In the end I was off for a year.
I had a final meeting.
30/8/2011.
I had no POA representation at the meeting. Apparently there were no POA reps in the North West available that day.
Mmmm, I wonder.
I paid into the POA every month, I was a POA rep as well.

All I ever got out of them was a bloody diary every year.
Thanks guys. Not.

It was with the then Deputy Governor, he was a nice enough
guy to deal with.
Also present a member of HR.
The meeting was in Preston.
They both asked if I was ok to which I said I was, bar the pain
I was going through and sometimes difficulty walking.
They looked at options.
Stay in the job with a possibility of lighter duties.
Medical Retirement or Medical inefficiency.

I thought about the options.
In the end I chose medical inefficiency.
I didn't want to return, as the Service was changing, not for the
better.
Medical retirement would make it hard for me to find work in
the future should my injury heal.
A lot of employers think you'll be no good if you've been
medically retired.
Medical inefficiency meant I'd have chance of working again.
I actually shed a tear as I signed to say I was finished.
I don't know why , but I was a bit upset.
Probably thinking that I'd given all that time to a job and this
was goodbye.

The Deputy Governor said to me.
" Tony, you will be missed , you were a damn good Officer
from a staff and Prisoner perspective"
He thanked me for my Service and I left the room.
The drive back to the Wirral was a strange one.
I was unemployed now, with an injury.
It was a daunting thought.

There was no going back.

A massive thank you to all at HMP Haverigg.
Not an easy jail to work at.
Please stay safe guys.

Waterfalls.

The reason I called this book
" Prison walls to Waterfalls" is what happened after I'd left the service.

I took a trip up to Scotland to visit family.
I drove up to a place called
" The Hermitage" about 12 miles up the A9 from Perth near the lovely little town of Dunkeld in Perthshire.
We used to go up there as kids with my parents. The place is absolutely stunning.
There is a place there where you can sit and watch the Waterfall.
I sat at the beautiful Waterfall up there quietly on my own.
Thinking.
I was no longer a Prison Officer.
I was Free.

If I could sum up my career as a Prison Officer I'd say
,Challenging, happy, sad, annoyed, content, discontent, humorous, scary, Violent,knackering, Adrenalin flowing, crazy, bloodcurdling, Teamwork, Camaraderie, manic, heartbreaking, piss taking, fulfilling, draining…

I could go on and on.
I think I felt every emotion known to man.
It took me over 6 years to get my emotions back.
You become hardened to everything.
My humour is as dark as a night sky.
What I find funny, many others would find highly offensive.
They call it Prison Humour as I've mentioned in the content of the book.

In the time I was in the Service PTSD wasn't a word.
I now hear of Officers diagnosed with this.
Guys, anyone fighting this now from the trauma of the job, I wish you a speedy recovery.
If needed, you know where I am.
I mean that with all sincerity.
Do not battle it alone.
To all I have served with, I wish and hope you are all well.
It was a Pleasure.

It is my belief by writing this book it has helped me deal with some of my demons from the service.
Yes, it's opened up some wounds, but it's helped me close them at the same time.

Over 16 and a half years behind 4 walls.
As well as prisoners doing time, so we're we.
Unless you've done it you wouldn't fully understand it.
No TV documentary can fully show it ,or capture all the emotions an Officer can go through.
You are a Prison Officer, a Social Worker, an Agony uncle or Aunt , a Goodie and a Baddie all in one days work.
Could you do it?
Would you want to do it?

The naughty 40.

Denise Livingstone.
Kim Evans
Steve Shepherd
Taff Howells
Terry Martin
Pete Codd
Barry Joyce
Rick Curson
Karl Grimshaw
Paul Wilcox
Mark Loft
Mia Walker
Mark Harris
Jason Delahaye
Kev Jess
Alan Melrose
Dawn Bickerdyke
Davina Cunnington
Andrea Parton
Mark Harper
Aubrey Thomas
Clive Moreland
Allan Clarke
Nigel Link.
Emma Matthews
Lesley Andrews
Miranda Playford

Tom White
Clayton Brownlow
Shane Peel
Steve Loveley
Stewart Stevens
James Cowie
Mel Holmes
Pete Wing
Gav Moore
Rob Seager.
Me
And one that I can't remember the name.

About the author.

I spent my early years in a few different places.
My Father was a Soldier so we moved around a bit.
Finally we settled in Perth when my father joined the Scottish
Prison Service.
I left school and became a hairdresser in Perth.
In 1995 I joined Her Majesty's Prison Service as a Prison
Officer.
I left through injury in August 2011.

Since then I've had varying jobs and was heavily involved in
Liverpools Music scene including playing Bass guitar in a
signed band.
I returned to Scotland in 2017.

I live in Edinburgh with my Partner Sarah and her two children.
I now work with Teenagers and adults with extra educational support needs.
I teach art and music with them.

Printed in Great Britain
by Amazon

17231776R00077